To

Duncan

April 2008.

My Mission Statement

To empower you to achieve your goals by questioning and measuring your financial life planning.

The WealthFlow System

The WealthFlow System is a positive commitment to guide and educate. By creating a system that can be monitored over many years, significant progress towards financial freedom can be made.

Duncan R Glassey CFP AIFP MSFA, The WealthFlow Partnership

"This book is a simple, witty and thought provoking explanation of the financial planning process. It is aimed at ordinary people and will help them to understand their financial aspirations or concerns. It deals with fundamental issues and attitudes not just the boring numbers. Written in layman's English rather than technical jargon, it should be compulsory reading for all financial planners as well as their clients."

PAUL GRAINGER
CERTIFIED FINANCIAL PLANNER LICENCE SENIOR ASSESSOR, UK

"Financial Freedom is a great introduction to Life Planning, the most dynamic, client-oriented movement in the financial planning profession today. A valuable resource for both the general public and the professional alike."

GEORGE KINDER, FOUNDER OF THE KINDER INSTITUTE OF LIFE PLANNING
AND AUTHOR OF THE SEVEN STAGES OF MONEY MATURITY

"Our weakness is that we all too often follow the herd, we see this all around us from the clothes we wear, the cars we drive to the stocks that we invest in, unfortunately following the herd can often result in losing sight of what our goals in life are. Financial Freedom empowers the reader with the clarity of vision to determine ones' true personal goals. Unlike many books of its genre, Financial Freedom reinforces its message in an interesting and entertaining way with its metaphors, anecdotes, and investment principles. Because of the ease with which you can read this book, it is a must read for all."

ALEXANDER LINTON, VICE PRESIDENT
INTERNATIONAL INVESTMENT BANK, 10 YEARS EXPERIENCE ON WALL STREET AND CITY OF LONDON

"Financial Planning is relatively simple really, spend less than you earn and sensibly accumulate the difference. The reality is often more complex than this. The WealthFlow System used by Duncan R Glassey is a guide to coach you via a simple and yet empowering process to achieving your goals and realising your lifestyle ambitions. Financial Freedom is all about making the Seven Habits of Financial Freedom ingrained in your thinking and making Financial Life Planning second nature. I wholeheartedly endorse this book as a must read for anyone who is serious about embracing much wider concepts about life planning than simply living from paycheck to paycheck."

KEVIN BAILEY CFP
FOUNDER, THE MONEY MANAGERS LTD
MELBOURNE, AUSTRALIA

FINANCIAL FREEDOM
USING THE W€althFlow™ SYSTEM

DUNCAN R GLASSEY CFP

Copyright Duncan R Glassey © 2004

Published by The WealthFlow Partnership Ltd
www.wealthflow.org

ISBN 0-9549090-0-3
Author: Duncan R Glassey
Editor: Fiona Cowan at Summertime Publishing
www.summertimepublishing.com

Cover / Interior design: Derrick Leung
Printed in the United Kingdom

AdvisorPress
1153 Bordeaux Drive, Suite 109
Sunnyvale, CA 94089
001 408 400 0400
www.advisorpress.com

Preface

Many of us find money to be a difficult area in our lives. We may achieve much success in other aspects of what we do and yet we know that we do not manage our finances as well as we should. Many of us have not had a financial education. We do not understand how money fits in with our hopes, dreams and aspirations. We neglect our financial health, knowing that in some way we ought to be doing more but deferring action until... well, until some time in the future. We manage to separate our money from our lives - but not to manage our money.

Duncan Glassey sets out to address the financial challenges which face many of us. Ingrained habits are difficult to change. He understands how difficult it is for us. He understands that traditional approaches to financial advice do not work for many of us. He seeks to place money and its consequences in the wider context of our overall lives. He offers to act as our guide and companion along the way. He has produced a set of tools which, if we linger long enough to use them, may transform our approach to our money – and, as a result, transform our lives. Duncan offers no magic solution. But the ideas in this book are what many of us need if we are to free ourselves from the nagging uncertainty about our financial futures.

I have known Duncan Glassey for a number of years. He has advised my family and myself through interesting and changing times. He has made us more aware of our financial health and of the remedies available to us if we are to improve upon it. It is, of course, still up to us. But Duncan's holistic approach and friendly support has made the journey an easier one to make. And Duncan has been prepared to make his own journey, moving from a secure and well paid job to the adventure of writing this book, because he has a vision that we can all manage our money more effectively. For that he deserves respect and admiration. Throughout, and this is the real test, Duncan models in his own behaviour what he suggests to others.

I commend this book. Using it effectively will take perserverence. However, years from now when many of us look back, we may have Duncan Glassey to thank for helping us to find financial health and the wellbeing that comes with financial security.

Professor John Sturrock QC
Chief Executive,
Core Solutions Group, Edinburgh
November 2004

Foreword

For a long time my career was fun, working for large actuarial, accountancy and legal practices. But that type of environment has unforeseen consequences. Slowly, I became weary of chasing after the right clients, the right image and the right income, and ultimately began to question the assumption that *more* is always *better*.

As I thought about this, I noticed that I most enjoyed working with people who were committed to self improvement. I loved to engage with them about their life, not just their money.

For a long time I have known that my ability to connect with others is dependent upon how well I know myself. I've attended courses run by top business schools and the UK's best financial planners. During those years I attained numerous financial planning qualifications, finally becoming a Certified Financial Planner (CFP) in 2003. CFP® is the worldwide benchmark for financial planning professionals.

The acronym CFP, the term Certified Financial Planner, and the CFP flame logo are licence marks, and are licensed to the Institute of Financial Planning (IFP). The IFP can help you find financial planners who are committed to competent and ethical behaviour when providing financial planning advice.

Individuals certified by the IFP have taken that extra step to demonstrate their professionalism, by voluntarily submitting to the rigorous CFP licence process. This includes highly demanding education, examination, experience and ethical requirements.

To broaden my education and outlook on life, I moved outside the field of financial planning. I trained as a mediator and re-established my religious faith. All of this has increased my capacity to work intimately with people and has helped me to revise and radically rethink my approach to financial planning.

Going a step further, and with the explicit permission of my family, I reorganised my life and now work with a small number of clients, many of whom have become close personal friends. These changes have allowed me to focus on what I really care about — being with others, authentically and compassionately, in order to help them take back control of their money, and to build fuller and more meaningful lives.

My wife, Colette, and I live with our children in a beautiful part of Central Scotland with views towards Stirling Castle, the Wallace Monument, the Ochil Hills, out across the Firth of Forth, as far as Fife and right along the coast towards Edinburgh.

While many financial planners focus on a narrow range of issues, I advocate *holistic* financial life planning and the value of long-term relationships. I want to understand your needs and goals, and lead you through some often confusing and difficult conversations about money and its role in your life. That way, we can work together to assemble a sustainable and valuable financial plan to deliver what you are looking for.

In setting up my own business, my mission was to empower people to achieve their goals by questioning and measuring their financial life. As the owner, I am dedicated to supporting people in understanding and using money, so they can contribute to their families and communities and lead rich, satisfying lives.

Working on a fee-only basis, I work solely for my clients. In other words, I don't sell any financial products in order to get paid. This eliminates any conflicts of interest regarding where my pay comes from or how I evaluate a client's financial options. Because I consider financial planning to be a dynamic process, I encourage my clients to call, email or visit me, in addition to our scheduled appointments, at no extra cost.

My career goal is to help develop financial life planning in the UK. I plan to work in partnership with my clients in order to integrate money and life. That's why I developed The WealthFlow System, a process based on 10 years of research, experiment and experience of advising some of the UK's most successful people.

Perhaps the key to the whole system is the *integrated approach* to financial planning, which allows you to view the big picture.

In this book, we will examine issues ranging from lifestyle… to pension needs… and educational ambitions for children and grandchildren. Going through this searching process will give you a greater insight into your needs and desires. It will help create an understanding of your past, present and future plans, as they relate to your career goals, life goals and financial goals. Only by dealing with these questions can your financial advisers know you well enough to be able to coach you through the vast array of financial decisions you will make during your lifetime.

Goal-setting sessions should include an in-depth discussion of your present situation. This includes assets, liabilities, income, expenses, potential income and estate taxes, plans for distribution of assets, existing trust agreements, Wills, investments, insurance, personal and family obligations and employer-sponsored benefit programmes.

A written plan can then be tailored to your individual needs, including the following:

- Goal-Setting
  (Chapter One: Progressive Life Planning & Management)

- Cash Flow Management
  (Chapter Two: Breakthrough Cash & Credit Management)

- Risk Management & Insurance
  (Chapter Three: Personal Risk Management Programme)

- Investment Planning
  (Chapter Four: Savings, Investment & Risk Integration)

- Retirement Planning
  (Chapter Five: Retirement & Life Transition Management)

- Tax Planning
  (Chapter Six: Tax Planning & Mitigation Programme)

- Estate Planning
  (Chapter Seven: Estate Planning & Management Programme)

Using this system, you will see the importance of clarifying exactly what you want from your money, your life and potentially from your professional advisers. Rather than simply monitoring performance as the major determinant to achieving your financial objectives, you will decide which objectives you actually want to achieve, thus giving your money real value and creating personal motivation.

Duncan R Glassey

Credentials

Duncan R Glassey CFP AIFP MSFA is the founding principal of The WealthFlow Partnership. He specialises in holistic personal financial planning with an emphasis on life planning.

Prior to establishing The WealthFlow Partnership, Duncan was Personal Financial Planning Director at Scotland's leading private client law firm. A category winner of Planned Savings Magazine's Financial Planner of the Year 2000 (category: Investment and Investment Planning), he serves on the Scottish branch committee of the Institute of Financial Planning.

Duncan R Glassey is an Associate of the Institute of Financial Planning, a member of the Society of Financial Advisers (The Personal Finance Society), a pension transfer specialist, an accredited mediator, and is one of the few Scots to hold the internationally recognised Certified Financial Planner (CFP) Licence.

Acknowledgements

This book is dedicated to my father, who taught me to work hard, and to my mother for her limitless belief in me. Also to my sister, for her continuing support.

A great many people had a hand in shaping this work and making me the person I am. I wish to thank them all. All that is written in these pages, I have learned from the people I have worked for and those I have worked with, and from the friends and family I'm so privileged to have.

It's motivating to be part of a profession that is excited about learning, and generous about sharing knowledge.

Thank you to colleagues Haig Bathgate and Ian Kennedy for their devotion to creating a better model; to US planner Nancy Langdon Jones and commentator Bob Veres for their inspiring views and foresight; to Paul Etheridge, George Kinder, Mitch Anthony and David Norton – true pioneers of financial life planning.

Thanks to Terrence O'Halloran for helping me find my editor, Fiona Cowan, who brought a reassuring commitment to getting this material together and on time; for her thoughtfulness and values; to Kenny Kemp for his encouragement.

Special thanks to Judy Lawrence of AdvisorPress for taking forward my ideas with vigour, and to the AdvisorPress team led by Peter W Johnson, Jason Papier and Mattias Bergman.

My appreciation extends to the many wonderful clients who freely shared their experiences and insights. In particular, to Prof. John Sturrock QC for his mentoring and kind heart, thank you.

Finally, a heartfelt thank you to my wife Colette for creating the environment to turn this book from thought to reality. I pray that we all continue to live this wonderful life.

Duncan R Glassey

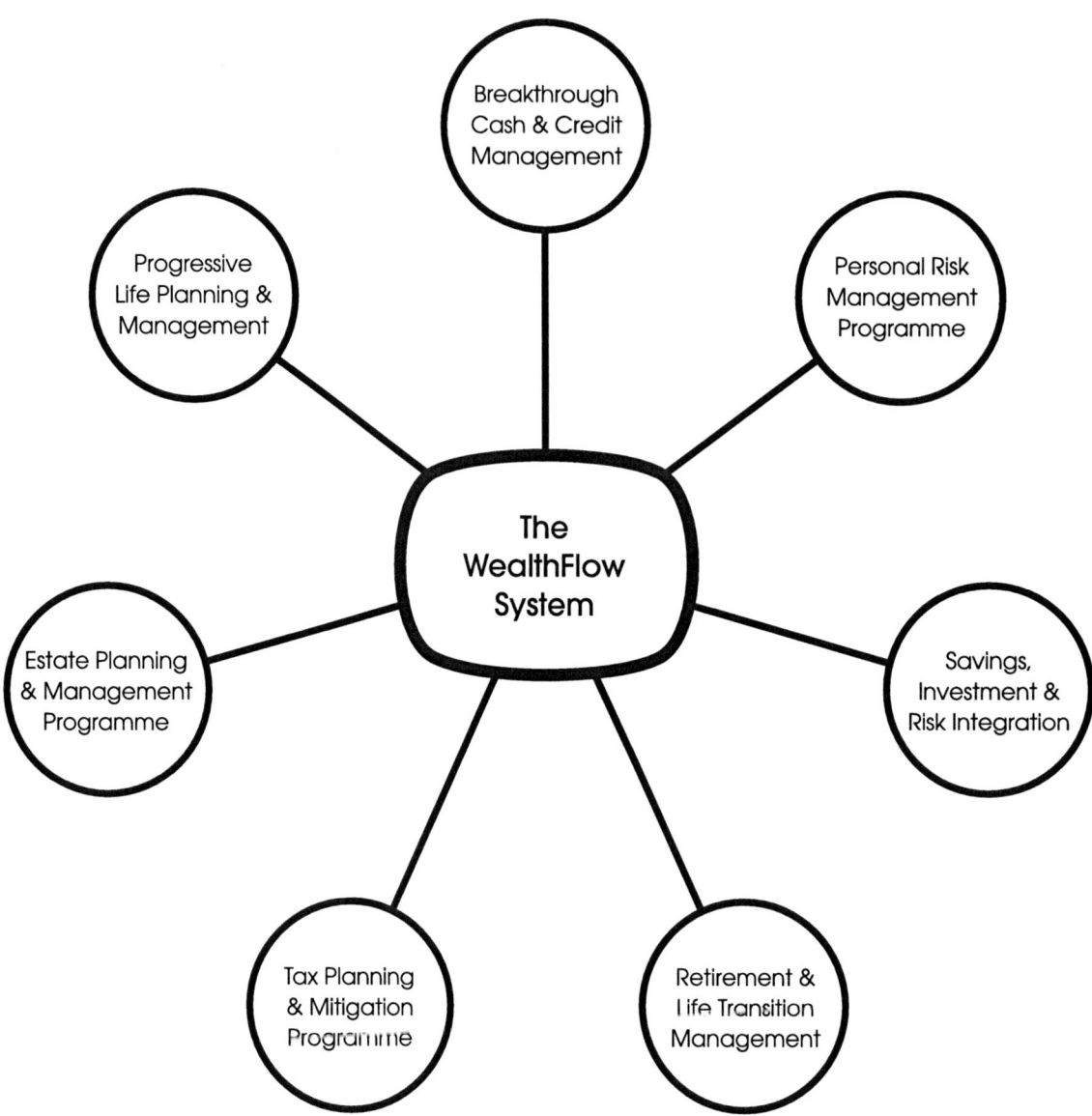

wealth

The stock of assets accumulated by individuals, households, businesses or nations. These assets can be physical possessions (for example, land or buildings), financial assets (bank accounts and securities) or 'human capital' (people's skills and talents).

flow

To move along steadily and continuously showing no sign of stopping.

system

A set of connected parts forming a complex whole; an organised scheme or method.

SOURCE: THE NEW OXFORD DICTIONARY

Contents

Introduction

Have you decided that you don't want to handle all your financial stuff on your own? Do you want direction and support?

If you are not yet where you want to be financially, maybe it's time for you to get focused, and create peace of mind about this essential part of your life.

You may be anticipating or recovering from one or more of life's transitions. Whether it's a change of career path, receiving an inheritance, entering a marriage, contemplating a divorce, facing redundancy, bankruptcy, illness or bereavement — this book is written for you.

The idea is radical and new, based upon something I call The WealthFlow System. It's a cyclical process that links your life objectives with quantifiable results. The system is designed for people who want to develop a coherent plan for achieving a better life. It enables clients and professional advisers alike to focus on what truly matters in financial planning — helping to establish goals, and to chart your progress in achieving them.

Few people are truly satisfied with their professional advisers. So, the process embodied in The WealthFlow System encourages people just like you to design and develop successful long-term client/adviser relationships. As you follow the steps, you will question the past, present and future direction of your financial life. You will uncover your long-term goals and future purpose, and begin working towards achieving them in real life.

Financial life planning is a continuous system of refinement. It needs close monitoring and adjustment to ensure you remain focused on what you want from life. This book is the first financial life planning tool of its kind.

You will discover how to:

- clarify what success means to you
- track and measure financial success
- feel more comfortable around money
- work better with your professional advisers

Effective life planning doesn't have to be a lonely journey. With the proper guide, it can be an exciting adventure of self-discovery, leading to clarification of future goals and greater financial security. I would like to be your guide.

'I have climbed my mountain, but I must still live my life.'

TENZING NORGAY
1914–1986, SHERPA GUIDE

Duncan R Glassey

Progressive Life Planning and Management | CHAPTER 01

> *'The importance of money flows from it being a link between the present and the future.'*
>
> JOHN MAYNARD KEYNES
> 1883-1946, ECONOMIST

The material contained within these pages has the potential to change your life forever. Many people have told me it has been the turning point for them. My goal is that this book will be the turning point for you.

It's strange how difficult people find it to decide what they want in life. You would think it the easiest thing in the world, because we're constantly concerned with ourselves. We're always interested in how much we can get, how well we can perform, how comfortable we can be.

So with all that, why is it so difficult to decide our own future?

> *'Let the beauty you love be what you do.'*
>
> MOWLANA JALALUDDIN RUMI
> 1207-1273, SUFI POET

The WealthFlow System (WFS) is based upon the goals you wish to achieve and the person you wish to become. The questions posed at the end of each chapter are vital elements of the WFS. Most people want more, but find it hard to define what the 'more' is.

When people do have goals, they often define them in material terms — for example, a larger house, a better job, more money, a luxury car. It is more unusual to find someone who knows how to make life more meaningful and how to improve relationships with others.

Most of us are under the delusion that we act freely. In truth, we are often enslaved to our egos and to ego-based aspects of our materialistic lifestyle. We are held captive by our jobs, our mortgages, our clothes or our need to outdo others. The WFS will provide the wisdom and strength to resist trading life's true pleasures — family, friendship, children and spiritual fulfilment — for the fleeting pleasures associated with gratifying our own egos.

Having the confidence to decide our future is rare, perhaps because we already know quite a few things about ourselves which need to be 'fixed' before we embark on our own journey. It's so much easier to help someone else achieve their objectives than to face the risks of setting our own. It will come as no surprise that this lack of confidence may be detrimental to our own personal growth.

In George Kinder's seminal work *The Seven Stages of Money Maturity* (Dell Publishing), he refers to the teaching stories of the Sufis, the mystic branch of Islam. Kinder says: 'The character of Nazrudin figures as the holy trickster, the wild man who upends people's blinkered, conventional ways of thinking and forces them to look at themselves anew.'

Think of Nazrudin as a man of basic means, whose lack of formal education is compensated by his basic streetwise cunning. Few people can be sure whether he is fool or genius. He is a legendary figure in Central Asian folklore. Stories about him abound, from Afghanistan to Turkey.

I have chosen to include some of his stories because Nazrudin always combines humour with a serious theme. He does not reflect my own religious views — and that is exactly why I chose him. I hope the often hidden messages of a stranger, Nazrudin, will bring you lighthearted relief during this book. As you read each story, ask yourself: *who is really the fool?*

I might just as easily have chosen Till Eulenspiegel, a German folk hero of the 14th century, another peasant trickster whose jokes and pranks became the source of many folk tales, exposing the foolishness of those who think themselves wiser than others. All of these tales are very old. The Till stories go back to before 1515, and Nazrudin's to before the 1300s. But these medieval urban legends are as fresh and revealing today as they ever were.

The humour is often slapstick, as the hapless and wily are able to get the better of kings, priests, landlords, shopkeepers, and anyone else in authority, generally by taking their statements literally. The name Eulenspiegel literally means 'owl mirror', and may refer to the proverb: *Man sees his own faults as little as a monkey or an owl recognises his ugliness on looking into a mirror.* Till is a comic anti-hero, holding up the mirror to man's foolishness.

As George Kinder relates: One of the many stories tells of the day Nazrudin went to the bank to cash a cheque. The bank teller examined the draft, looked at the Mullah, and said, "Can you identify yourself, sir?"

"Certainly," said the Mullah, without a moment's hesitation. He rummaged in his satchel and pulled out a small hand mirror, in which he admired his own face. Then the Mullah announced proudly, "That's me all right!"

This rather silly story highlights the need for us to seek out ways to help discover our own identity and to bring that discovery to bear in our own life. The Sufis say: *'If human beings knew their own inner secrets, never would they look elsewhere for seeking happiness, peace and inner light.'*

The truth of the matter is, we can only know ourselves in relation to others who hold up a mirror in which we see a reflection of ourselves in their eyes. Out of the many mirrors, reflecting various images of who we are, we weave a sense of self. Eventually, we choose which of those images we wish to claim as our authentic self.

> *'O wad some power the giftie gie us, to see oursels as ithers see us!'*
> *(O would some power the gift to give us, to see ourselves as others see us!)*
>
> ROBERT BURNS
> 1759-1796, SCOTLAND'S NATIONAL BARD

Clarity of thinking about who we are comes from asking ourselves the right questions. First comes *recognition* of our past, followed by the present, and then our future. Then comes *change*.

Recognition is the most difficult part for most people, because it is difficult to see what goes on inside of oneself. Most people wish for a secure financial future, constantly hoping for the best. However, the feeling of security arises when one sees reality inside of oneself and comes to terms with it. The inward focus is an important aspect of our financial life.

> *'Look abroad thro' nature's range, nature's mighty law is change.'*
>
> ROBERT BURNS

Today, many people are faced with having to deal with instant wealth and windfalls from a variety of sources. These may include inheritance, lump-sum retirement payouts, insurance settlements, divorce agreements and Lottery winnings.

Let's consider a Lottery winner's initial frame of mind. They can now buy everything they want for the rest of their lives. And so they buy a new house, a new car or two, they give money to relatives and friends, take regular trips, and within a few years they're resentful that 'the money' has somehow let them down.

It may come as no surprise that a survey of Lottery winners by the Camelot Group Plc, operator of The UK National Lottery, highlighted that, on the whole, these lucky people — while happier as a result of their winnings — are often frustrated that the money could have been better spent.

The WFS was created in order to measure your success in taking back control of your life and money. It is deeply rooted in some powerful questions:

- *If you suddenly found that you had only one day to live, what would be your biggest regret?*
- *If you had all the money in the world, how would you live your life differently from the way you do right now?*

Later in this chapter you will be asked to think through as many as 100 such questions, in order to get you really thinking about your past, present and future financial life. The goal is to empower you, and as a result of heightened self-awareness, improve the effectiveness of your working relationships with professional advisers.

The vast majority of successful people began right at the bottom. All we have to do is find out what these people did differently from us, do the same things, and presumably get the same results. We live in a universe governed by laws not chance.

A passage from Buddhist scripture (the Shinjikan Sutra) states: 'If you want to understand the causes that existed in the past, look at the results as they are manifested in the present. And if you want to understand what results will be manifested in the future, look at the causes that exist in the present.'

Traditional financial services have changed dramatically over the last 20 years. At one time people were happy simply to access investments, such as unit trusts, life and pension funds — things which had previously been available only to the very wealthy. Our objective now is **a better life, more understanding of goals and objectives, more integration of how money is used in relation to what you really want out of life.** Often, the greatest financial challenge is simply to increase cash flow in order to support this better life — *see Chapter Two: Breakthrough Cash & Credit Management.*

Financial life planning is new and dynamic. It is tied in with everything about your life that is important. The constant theme is exploration. It's about much more than beating the markets. A whole new kind of financial counsel has emerged.

The basic system of financial life planning is designed to create a forum in which you feel safe and free to explore your interests and possibilities. Three fundamental principles contribute to this situation:

- Financial life planning is voluntary and consensual
- Financial life planning is private and confidential
- Financial life planning is conducted without prejudice or hidden agendas

Financial life planning represents the human side of money — your identity.

The question is: *what is money all about?*

Is money something more personal than the balance of your bank account? Do your professional advisers truly know who you are? Delivering the lifetime you desire is the goal of life planning. So, what is the life worth living?

Financial life planning is an extraordinary subject, helping you uncover what you truly want from your life, and who you want to become. Then, it provides a system that helps you achieve those goals.

If we start out from the belief that *you ultimately become what you think about most of the time*, then it should come as no surprise that those who look ahead and plan their lives are the most successful. In my experience this is such a strong predictor that it transcends virtually all financial factors. It explains how someone earning an average income can save as much as, or even more than, someone on double that income.

This simple truth flies in the face of conventional wisdom, which suggests that financial success is simply a result of making more money. You must have a *clear vision* of what you are working towards, in order to motivate yourself. Successful people are very clear about who they are and what they want. Unsuccessful people are often confused and uncertain.

'Seek and ye shall find.'

BOOK OF MATTHEW

The WFS should help you reflect upon your financial life. Success must not simply be about 'rates of return'. Becoming financially independent is wonderful for the money, but it is *the person you have to become* that is most important of all.

To become an exemplary person financially, you must become an exemplary person!

Asking searching questions of yourself and of your lifestyle is at the heart of the system.

A husband/wife solicitor team are clients of mine, and they went through this process.

During the first session, before doing any number crunching, they completely reorganised their office hours. They recognised that they needed to address their work-life balance, so that each could spend more time with the children.

I have seen at first hand the difference between people who think about these questions and those who don't. Framing the right questions and raising the important issues is at the core of the WFS. The objective is to provide you with a life-changing experience.

Why do people hire professional advisers?

What do you really value? Knowing what you value is the core of any professional relationship. I am convinced, however, that most professional advisers are unclear about the deepest desires of their clients. They simply don't ask enough of the right questions. In my experience, you want to know how much your advisers care, rather than simply how much they know. A financial planning engagement needs to be far more personal than most advisers realise.

> *Once upon a time, a dervish and his student were walking down a long, quiet road. Suddenly, they saw dust rising in the distance. A fine carriage pulled by six horses approached at full gallop. The men soon realised that this carriage was not going to slow down or veer to avoid them. In fact it was coming upon them at such speed that they had to throw themselves from the road, landing unceremoniously in a ditch. The two men got up as quickly as they could and looked back at the carriage as it sped by.*
>
> *The student thought to curse, but not before the dervish called out to the carriage's occupants, 'May all of your deepest desires be satisfied!'*
>
> *'What?' exclaimed the mystified student. 'Why would you wish something so good for those men? They just forced us into the ditch — we could have been hurt.'*
>
> *'Do you really think,' replied the dervish, 'that if their deepest desires were satisfied, they would go around treating others as they treated us?'*

The WFS is a tool to help you get what you want. Think of it as a coaching tool to help you focus on where you are, what's important to you and where you're headed.

In any relationship, clarity is key. Perhaps this is why many people have lost faith in traditional financial services. Supported by complex products with ambiguous charging structures, they worry rather than empower people.

The questioning and goal-setting associated with the WFS is an all-year-round process. It should be discussed at every meeting with your professional advisers, typically four to six times a year. This allows you to keep on top of your objectives. The professional adviser's role is to hold you accountable, answer questions and help you to work through obstacles.

The WFS is rooted in the belief that setting purely financial objectives, without truly understanding your beliefs, values and motivations, is pretty meaningless. Although many of your concerns will be money-orientated, self discovery often has little to do with attaining vast sums of money.

Success, I believe, is composed of four ingredients:

- Health and Energy
- Loving Relationships
- Meaningful Work (man's need for meaning and purpose)
- Financial Independence (we need to have enough so that we do not worry)

In achieving financial independence, you must understand the practicalities of financial planning, which I call The Big Six:

    i.   Cash Flow Management
    ii.   Risk Management & Insurance
    iii. Investment Planning
    iv. Retirement Planning
    v.   Tax Planning
    vi. Estate Planning

In practice, if you are working with a professional adviser, your success should be monitored at regular, perhaps quarterly meetings. This allows you to review goals and chart your progress.

Professional advisers should not make judgements on your goals. In Sufism, Nazrudin taught that what people see as truth is relative only to their own situation.

There once was a dervish devotee who believed that it was his task to reproach those whose goals he considered inappropriate, and to ensure that they find the right path. What this devotee did not know, however, was that a true teacher does not apply the same fixed principles to everyone. Unless the teacher knows exactly what is in the heart of the student, the teacher may achieve the opposite of what he or she desires.

However, one day this particular devotee came upon a man who gambled excessively and who did not know how to stop. The devotee decided to intervene, and started to monitor the gambler. Every time the gambler went to the gambling den, the devotee placed a stone in a pile outside the gambler's house to mark the sin, so that the growing pile would accumulate as a visible reminder of evil.

And so, each time the gambler left his house for the gambling den, he felt guilty. Each time he returned, he felt worse, as the pile of stones had grown.

This process continued for twenty years. And each time the gambler saw the devotee, he said to himself, 'How that saintly man works for my redemption. He is sure of his place in heaven.'

It so happened that, through a natural catastrophe, both men died at the same time. An angel came to the gambler and said to him, gently, 'You are to come with me to Paradise.'

The gambler protested, saying, 'How can that be? I am a sinner and must go to Hell. Surely you must be here for the devotee who has tried to reform me for the last two decades?'

But the angel replied, 'The devotee? No, he is being taken to the lower regions as we speak.'

'What justice is this?' shouted the gambler, forgetting his situation. 'You must have got your instructions reversed,' he added.

'Not so,' said the angel. 'This is how things stand: for twenty years, the devotee has been indulging himself with feelings of superiority and merit. He ended up putting those stones on that pile for himself, not for you, and now he must redress the balance.'

'And how have I earned a reward?' asked the gambler.

> *'You are to be rewarded because every time you passed the devotee, you longed first for goodness, and then thought of the devotee in a charitable way. It is goodness which is rewarding you for your fidelity.'*

The Sufis are convinced that it is not what facts you know, but *how well you know yourself*, that counts.

Do not let other people judge what is right for you. Instead, share who you are, and your dreams, with like-minded individuals who accept and encourage you.

> *'Keep your fears to yourself, but share your courage with others.'*
>
> ROBERT LOUIS STEVENSON
> 1850-1894, SCOTTISH AUTHOR

Financial life planning is not about *fixing stuff*. It's about letting you achieve what is important to you. The money is simply there to help you along the way.

It is your responsibility to achieve a life you truly want. If you want to spend more time with your family, then you simply don't work as much. This is where you and your professional advisers must find the additional money. When you get married or divorced, when you decide where you are going to live, money is always an issue.

Personal experience has shown me that the strongest professional relationships centre around the success of financial life planning over traditional financial services. This new paradigm is far more akin to personal mentoring. Like a game of chess, financial life planning is at times more art than science.

> *'Not all artists may be chess players, but all chess players are artists.'*
>
> MARCEL DUCHAMP
> 1887-1968, FRENCH/AMERICAN CONCEPTUAL ARTIST

Often, experience is more important than mere answers.

> *One day a seeker, after a lengthy and difficult search, found Nazrudin sitting in a hut on the side of a mountain. Knowing that every action of the illuminated Sufi was important, the seeker asked why Nazrudin was blowing on his hands.*
>
> *'They're cold, so I'm warming them,' Nazrudin replied.*
>
> *A little while later, Nazrudin produced two bowls of soup, and began to blow on his own. Again, the seeker asked why, and this time Nazrudin explained he was cooling it.*

With that, the seeker left, unable to trust any longer a man who uses the same process to arrive at opposite results.

But of course, that is one of the first things that a financial life planner would want to convey — that the same process *can* give opposite results.

As I said earlier in this chapter, the Camelot Group Plc, operator of The UK National Lottery, released the first ever major survey of National Lottery winners to discover what effect winning the Lottery has on happiness, lifestyles and relationships. It makes interesting reading from a life planning perspective.

This survey gives a uniquely historic insight into the lives of Lottery winners over five years.
- 55% are happier after winning
- 43% experience no effect on happiness
- 2% are less happy after winning

The happiness of the winner is not affected by the size of his or her win.

Of the 55% of winners who are happier:
- 65% claim the reasons are improved financial security and fewer worries
- 23% say they can buy what they want and that life is a lot easier

There are no negative effects on family life or friendships:
- 95% remained married after winning
- 100% who were living with a partner prior to their win (but not married) are still in the same relationship

Friends:
- 90% of winners who already had a best friend before winning are still best friends with the same person

Food shopping habits:
- 37% of winners still buy supermarket own brands, regardless of the size of the win
- 4% claim to have switched from buying supermarket brands to individual brands

Work:
- 48% of all winners who were in regular work before their win are still in the same job

Winning the Lottery appears to have very little impact on the winners' perception of their social class or their political persuasion:
- 52% of winners of £ 2 million or more consider themselves to be working class, compared with 60% before their win
- 88% of Lottery winners still participate in the Lottery every week
- 2% of winners have stopped playing altogether

SOURCE: MORI 1999

Often, people who aspire to great wealth do so under the perception that the money will change them for the better. Such misguided perceptions remind me of another tale of the Muslim folk-hero, Nazrudin.

> *When an illiterate man assumed him to be learned on account of his beautiful and expensive-looking turban, Nazrudin gave the turban to the man and suggested he could now read his own letters.*

The WFS will question your values. Even when you are being catapulted from one economic status to another, your lifetime beliefs and core values change much more slowly. Indeed, for some people, they may never change.

The following round of questions is not included within the WFS scoring system. These are very personal questions on which to reflect. You may choose not to answer all of these questions. However, they will enable you to analyse your current position and, if shared, allow your professional advisers to understand you better. Moving from your past, through to your present position, and finally to the future, you will recognise that your experiences to date have shaped your underlying beliefs and attitudes towards money.

By identifying our belief systems, we can discover what creates anxiety for us. Then we can work around the anxiety to let go of bad habits and create positive emotions around money. Once we know the place money should have in our lives, we can keep it in that place without giving it more or less energy than it deserves.

> *Kabbalah, the ancient Jewish tradition of mystical interpretation, reveals 'The Opponent' — the unseen cause of chaos in the human spirit.*
>
> *He is the voice that whispers to us: 'Eat cake now and diet tomorrow.' He creates anxiety. You tell yourself you will spend more quality time with your family — but something compels you to work a 70-hour week. Someone collapses in the street — but you convince yourself that someone else will phone an ambulance. You make a commitment to pay off personal loans and save regularly — but each month you are persuaded to treat yourself to something you don't need. You divulge a secret you promised to keep, you buy vitamins and fail to take them, you join a gym and never attend, you fail to show up at family gatherings or business networking events, you visit fast food outlets when you know your sedentary lifestyle won't enable you to burn off the surplus calories.*
>
> *The Opponent is shrewd. Without clarity of purpose in our lives we are his willing victims.*

Don't be put off by the personal nature of the questions asked throughout the WFS. This level of self-questioning is necessary in order to analyse what may prove to be years of financial self-neglect, misunderstanding and lost battles with 'The Opponent'.

Allow yourself two hours, without interruption, to go through the following 100 questions. Be honest and spontaneous. Do not ponder your answers, simply write down what springs to mind. There are no right or wrong answers and only you can decide whether or not to share these with others.

The Priorities column should be used to organise any obstacles that stand between you and your major goals. Aim to uncover the largest obstacle, the one that, if removed, would make the greatest impact on your life and help you move ahead more rapidly.

Before jumping in to overcome the obstacle, think about why it is there, and why you haven't overcome it already. Prioritising your goals should help focus your efforts. Place them in sequence. If it's a particular fear that is holding you back, ask yourself: how does this hold me back? How does this fear **help** me? What would I **gain** by eliminating this fear?

For me, the fear was not having enough money. I also thought that working hard was admirable and that long hours proved my commitment. But, commitment to what? What did I really want? I didn't know.

So, I took on opportunities that paid me the highest salary, often taking on work and dealing with people whose values were not aligned to my own. Looking back, I was choosing security over opportunity.

How this fear **helped** me was to work much longer and harder than the average person. I was more ambitious and determined. My fear drove me to study harder and attain more and more qualifications.

Then I asked myself: What would I **gain** by eliminating this fear? I recognised that I would be willing to earn less, in order to fulfil my own goals rather than those of an employer. I could, and would, start my own business. By prioritising my goals and analysing my fears, I found the clarity to create the life that I desired. And so can you.

Get into the habit of transforming your life. However busy you are, take 10 minutes each day and delve in and out of these questions; not because I'm telling you to, but because your future life is important and deserves your regular attention.

QUESTIONS: **Progressive Life Planning & Management**	Notes	Priorities
p a s t		
1. What money messages did you receive when you were growing up? For example: 'money doesn't grow on trees'; 'everyone has a price'; 'money is the root of all evil'; 'money can't buy happiness'.		
2. What has made you really happy?		
3. As a child, when did you start getting your own spending money? Did you earn it?		
4. What was the first piece of music you bought? How did the purchase make you feel?		
5. The most traumatic financial experience of your life was when _____ .		
6. Describe the work ethic of your mother or father.		
7. How has money helped in reaching your life goals?		
8. What money habits have moved you away from achieving personal goals?		
9. When you were young, did you consider your family to be rich, poor, or something else?		
10. Who in the past has influenced your attitudes to money?		

11.	What were you taught about money when you were growing up?		
12.	What did you learn about money when you were growing up?		
13.	When growing up, was money a taboo subject? A source of conflict? A positive energy?		
14.	What methods have you considered in order to track your spending?		
15.	People accumulate their financial resources in many ways. What is the source of your financial resources?		
16.	In the past, how have you defined success in your working life?		
17.	In the past, how have you defined success in your family life?		
18.	When growing up, was money directed towards you to reward, punish, control, buy your love, or for something else?		
19.	What have been your best financial decisions to date?		
	present		
20.	What are the activities that give you your greatest sense of meaning and purpose in life?		

21. Identify the biggest challenge facing you today.		
22. Describe your day-to-day work.		
23. What do you consider valuable about planning your future?		
24. Do you write down your goals and make individual plans for their achievement?		
25. What is important about money to you?		
26. Are there particular goals that you wish to achieve in respect of your local community?		
27. How appropriate is your lifestyle now, relative to the lifestyle you aspire to in retirement?		
28. If you had more time on your hands, what would you choose to do?		
29. If you could delegate some of life's responsibilities, which would you most like to give up?		
30. Do you have a role model for successful living? What do you think contributes to that person's success?		

31.	In your current financial life, do you consider yourself a spender or a saver?		
32.	In your present situation, do you avoid or worry about financial decisions?		
33.	Is money an 'issue' in your current relationship?		
34.	If you had much more money, what would you do differently?		
35.	When do you feel most frustrated?		
36.	What hobbies/activities do you plan to take up within the next five years?		
37.	Of all life's wonders, what do you value the most?		
38.	How have your views towards money changed over the years?		
39.	What have you always wanted to do but been afraid to attempt?		
40.	Are you satisfied with your current job/career?		

41.	Are you satisfied with the income/benefits you receive from your current job/career?		
42.	Are you satisfied with your spending habits?		
43.	Are you satisfied with your ability to meet your financial obligations?		
44.	List what you think and talk about most of the time.		
45.	Values: Rank the top five and throw away the others. o achievement o adventure o culture o authority o money o friendship o love o health o independence o integrity o philanthropy o recreation o spiritual growth o work o security o service o family o others (specify)	1. 2. 3. 4. 5.	
46.	List the things you would most like to achieve regarding your personal health and fitness.		
47.	What is the most important thing that your money gives you at the moment?		
48.	What charities are important to you?		
49.	Do you avoid talking to your partner about money because it's too stressful?		
50.	Do you think love will solve your money problems?		

51.	Are you using your money according to your values?		
52.	List any habits that you would like to give up (for example, smoking, buying CDs that you never get around to listening to).		
53.	When you look back on your life in thirty years' time, what would it take for you to consider your life successful?		
54.	One dream I've had that now seems financially unattainable is to _____ .		
55.	Which of the following best describes you most of the time? Rank the top five. o thorough o dependable o humorous o tactful o decisive o calm o assertive o energetic o ambitious o generous o serious o adventurous o flexible o cautious o sensitive o hard-working o logical o patient o adaptable o optimistic o relaxed o trusting o organized o enthusiastic o other _____	1. 2. 3. 4. 5.	
56.	Financially, others see me as _____ .		
57.	I feel most alive when _____ .		
58.	Of everything in the world, what would you most like to be doing right now? Where would you most like to be?		
59.	What's important about money to you right now?		

60.	I especially enjoy my career because it gives me the opportunity to (rank the top three): o be creative o take risks o be of service to others o express myself o solve problems o socialise o compete/win o work in a team o organize o learn o lead others o achieve financial security	1. 2. 3.	

f u t u r e

61.	What do you expect from your professional advisers?		
62.	What fears or dangers might stand in the way of accomplishing your objectives?		
63.	Who will be affected most by the financial decisions you make now and in the future?		
64.	Do you understand your partner's views on money?		
65.	Identify your biggest problem or source of negativity towards money.		
66.	Imagine your business and career are perfect, five years from now. With whom would you be working?		
67.	What kind of relationships would you have with the most important people in your life, five years from now, if everything were perfect in every respect?		
68.	What changes would you have to start making today in your diet, exercise routines and health habits to become physically fit sometime in the future?		

69.	What additional knowledge and skills will you have acquired, five years from now?		
70.	In what areas of your work do you wish to be recognised as being excellent?		
71.	If you could design the perfect year, what would you do differently on your weekends and holidays?		
72.	What qualities will you be best known for in the future, among the people who know you?		
73.	Look into the most difficult situation you are dealing with right now. What valuable lessons does it contain for the future?		
74.	How serious are you about teaching your children/ grandchildren about money?		
75.	Are there personal factors or circumstances that are holding you back from a successful life?		
76.	Are you concerned that your health may fail you in retirement?		
77.	In the future, how will you define 'balance' in your life?		
78.	How would your life change if you knew you had only two years to live?		

79.	My biggest conflicts around money are with my o parents o children o spouse *(tick one)*		
80.	If money were not an issue, would you still be in your current job/career/profession?		
81.	What do you really want to be, have and do?		
82.	If you suddenly discovered that you had two days to live, what would be your biggest regret?		
83.	It's a couple of years from now. You're having tea with some friends. Tell me what's happened in that two-year period?		
84.	List the ways in which you would like to advance your education or qualifications.		
85.	List the places and countries that you would most like to travel to and see.		
86.	List the major assets that you are yet to acquire (for example, holiday home, boat, paintings). Be very specific.		
87.	What are the things that would be fun to do? You may never get around to it, but it would be fun to learn/do.		
88.	Describe a typical day in your life — in retirement.		

89.	What will you miss most about your career when you finally retire?		
90.	What are your biggest fears about retirement?		
91.	What situations do you want to avoid in retirement?		
92.	I consider my biggest financial blind spot to be _____ .		
93.	What do you most look forward to about retirement?		
94.	What are the top three things you would like to achieve/experience in retirement?		
95.	What changes in lifestyle do you intend making in retirement?		
96.	How long do you think it will be before you're bored with retirement? Will you ever get bored?		
97.	List the things that you would most like to achieve regarding your finances (for example, to be better organised, to increase savings).		
98.	Describe your life's work. Explain why you're here.		

99.	How do you hope to be remembered?		

A personal plan for success!

	Challenges You Face	*Strategies to Overcome Challenges*
100.		

Personal Coaching Tips

Ensure that you understand, perhaps with the help of your professional advisers, the following key areas:

- The purpose of financial planning
- The role of a financial planner
- The process involved in financial planning
- The documents that will be required before advice can be given
- The need to set goals and make plans for their accomplishment
- The main topics that need to be considered when constructing a financial plan

Notes / Doodles

Breakthrough Cash and Credit Management | CHAPTER 02

'The unexamined life is not worth living.'

SOCRATES
469–399 BC, GREEK PHILOSOPHER

The truth is, most of us are not good with money. We were not taught these skills throughout our mainstream education. If we finally seek professional help in later life, we worry that financial advisers simply want to earn a commission investing our capital, rather than helping us take control of our daily spending.

Back at home, communication is vital to a family's cash and credit management. If you have a life partner, the questions posed in this chapter should be answered by each of you separately. Then, at a time when you won't be interrupted, evaluate your answers together. These questions are intended to enrich your discussion. They are not intended to become a source of friction. Use them as tools to understand past, present and future decisions and to empower you to address the difficult issues.

If you are single, take the time to reflect personally on your answers, perhaps discussing them with a close friend or professional adviser.

Nazrudin decided to sell his donkey. He took him to the market place and handed him over to the market crier.

'Sell this donkey for a good price,' he said. 'I'll give you five silver coins.' The broker took the donkey and started to shout out his traits.

'A donkey like this never came to this market before. You cannot find its kind anywhere else. Such a bargain! Pile on as much load as you want, this donkey can carry it. If you don't feed him for three days, he won't complain. His strength won't be any less. He is not stubborn. You pull him this way, he goes this way, you pull him that way, he goes that way. He yields, shows no obstinacy. He can fly like a bird. You can drink your coffee on him when he is trotting...'

As the hawker praised the donkey thus, the buyers lined up. The price started to increase. Nazrudin was surprised to see all these people raising the bid for his donkey. He hadn't known that his animal had so many qualities. He decided to keep him after all. He paid the crier's fee and took the donkey back home.

When Nazrudin arrived home, he told his wife what had happened. She agreed that he had done the smart thing by paying the hawker and taking his donkey back.

'Today, I made a profitable deal, too,' she started to recount. 'The salt seller was passing by. I told him that we had some wheat to exchange for salt. He agreed, so we put the sack of wheat on one scale and the sack of salt on the other scale. But our wheat came up short. So, when the man was not looking, I slipped my two golden bracelets into the wheat sack. That way I was able to get even more salt. The salt seller picked up the wheat sack and left without doubting anything.'

Nazrudin stroked his long white beard contentedly. 'Wife,' he said, 'I from outside, you from inside, we are managing this house pretty well.'

A financial planning myth that is widely believed is that if you simply make more money, create more income, you'll be well on your way to riches. In Sufism, the mystical strand of Islam, many stories are told to create a suspicion of the too-easy answer. Sufis argue that everyone needs a new approach to break out of the way they have been conditioned to see things, so that they may come closer to seeing things as they really are.

A dervish was praying silently. A wealthy merchant, observing the dervish's devotion and sincerity, was deeply touched. The merchant offered the dervish a bag of gold. 'I know that you will use the money for God's sake. Please take it,' said the merchant.

'Just a moment,' the dervish replied. 'I'm not sure if it is lawful for me to take your money. Are you a wealthy man? Do you have more money at home?'

'Oh yes. I have at least a thousand gold pieces at home,' claimed the merchant proudly.

'Do you want a thousand gold pieces more?' asked the dervish.

'Why yes, of course. Every day I work hard to earn more money.'

'And do you wish for a thousand gold pieces beyond that?' asked the dervish.

'Certainly,' said the merchant. 'Every day I pray that I may earn more and more money.'

The dervish pushed the bag of gold back to the merchant. 'I am sorry, but I cannot take your gold,' he said. 'A wealthy man cannot take money from a beggar.'

'How can you call yourself a wealthy man and me a beggar?' the merchant spluttered.

The dervish replied, 'I am a wealthy man because I am content with whatever God sends me. You are a beggar, because no matter how much you possess, you are always dissatisfied, and are always begging God for more.'

The truth is that most people don't have an income problem — they have a spending problem. If you want to take a single message from this chapter, remember: *'It's not what you earn that determines your financial future, it's all about how much, or how little, you keep!'*

Ultimately, you may need to resort to a spending plan within which you can live. The majority of middle-class or wealthy people have spending problems, sometimes chronic enough to destroy their chances of having secure financial futures. So you are not alone.

'Our main business is not to see what lies dimly at a distance, but to do what lies clearly at hand.'

THOMAS CARLYLE
1795-1881, SCOTTISH AUTHOR, ESSAYIST AND HISTORIAN

An effective approach is to break the problem into bite-sized reviews, either on your own or with your professional adviser, once a week for the first month. As your situation improves, it drops to twice, and then once, a month. To ensure that you are committed to change, expect to pay for these sessions. The sooner your spending habits improve, the more you save in fees. Think of your planner as a counselor helping you develop a spending plan. The tools to empower are there, but you must take ultimate responsibility.

This brings us back to the basics of financial life planning. Its value is in helping the majority who work very hard, but never raise their heads to figure out what it is they really want. Few people give themselves permission to do this. Consider those who suddenly come into money for the first time, and who go out and buy a larger home in a better area. In reality, they may not want a larger home at all. They may want something completely different. But until they get help, they don't know it.

Let's face it, if you don't address how you handle money today, the best-laid plans for tomorrow will not come together. Financial life planning brings accountability, and with accountability comes motivation. It provides someone to report to every month and a system to lessen the pain. It encourages you to decide what's truly important to you, and what success means to you. Such decisions will allow you to put controls and limits on your own behavior, because now there's something bigger to work towards.

Paying close attention to your core values in order to rein in your money habits is important. If you haven't done so already, take this opportunity to rank in order of importance your top five values, discarding the others — see Chapter One: Progressive Life Planning & Management, question 45.

By focusing on your values, and therefore on what is truly important to you, you can begin to make choices about how you spend money. You will probably discover that you are spending a lot on things that you don't find fulfilling at all, other than the initial buzz of buying something new, the quick fix.

To begin, you may wish to draw up a detailed list of your spending habits during the last six months. Based on what the numbers show, and what you think you want to achieve, you can then identify changes that will enable you to achieve your goals. Reviewing bank statements is relatively straightforward. It's the cash withdrawals that will inevitably require some detective work.

In preparing this chapter, I came across a story that highlights our own inability to address the real issues, preferring instead to look elsewhere for solutions. The story I refer to originates from Sufi teachings.

One dark night, Nazrudin was on his hands and knees under a lamp, searching for something. A group of his neighbours came over to see what was happening.

'What have you lost, Nazrudin?' said one of his neighbours.

'My door key.'

The others got down on their hands and knees and searched for the key. After a long and unsuccessful search, one said, 'We've looked everywhere. Are you sure you dropped it here?'

Nazrudin looked him in the eye and answered, 'Of course I didn't drop it here. I dropped it outside my door.'

'Then why are you looking for it here?' one snapped.

'Obviously,' he said, 'because there's more light here.'

This story has personal relevance. No matter how much easier it is to search for something in the wrong place, you will never find it there. Unless you look in the right place, even if to do so is much more difficult, you will not find what you are looking for.

Not addressing our daily expenditure, but chasing higher investment returns, is one such example. In the UK this has manifested itself in the ability to remortgage one's home to release capital to fund our spending habits, rather than reduce monthly outgoings. We rely on sustained house price increases to maintain our delusional state.

The fight between saving and spending could be described as an epic saga. It tells us about ourselves. Writers and poets have always told human beings about themselves. Mostly people don't listen, because it doesn't help when somebody else tells us what's wrong with us — and few of us care to hear it.

Everybody wants to be somebody, and all too often that means owning stuff. It seems negative and depressing to be nobody and have nothing. We have to find out for ourselves that taking control of our finances can be exhilarating and liberating.

Perhaps you will never really be on top of your finances. Why? Because nobody really wants to say no to those little, and large, financial treats. It feels as if none of our friends or colleagues are ready to curtail their spending. But have we ever looked to see whether we, ourselves, have actually reduced our spending? When we haven't done so, why do we wonder that nobody else is ready for it either? Nobody wants to be the first one without the trophies of success.

Does it really matter? Who is that person who needs more? That 'more' is never ending.

Ramana Maharshi, a sage in southern India, said: *'Peace and happiness are not our birthright. Whoever has attained them has done so by continual effort.'*

There is a well-known metaphor about a monkey trap, the kind used in Asia which is a wooden funnel with a small opening. At the bigger end lies a sweet. The monkey, attracted by the sweet, puts his paw into the narrow opening and gets hold of the sweet. When he wants to draw his paw out again, he can't get his fist holding the sweet through the narrow opening. He is trapped and the hunter will come and capture him. He doesn't realise that all he has to do to be free is to let go of the sweet.

That's our financial life: a trap, because we want it nice and sweet. Not being able to let go, we're caught in the ever recurring happiness-unhappiness, up-down, hoping-despairing cycle. Instead of trying for ourselves, whether we could let go and be free, we resist and reject such a notion. Yet we all agree that all that matters is peace and happiness, which can only exist when we are free of financial worry.

One day, Nazrudin sent one of his disciples to the market to buy him a bag of chillies. The disciple did as requested and brought the bag to Nazrudin, who began to eat the chillies, one after another. Soon his face turned red, his nose started running, his eyes began to water and he was choking.

The disciple observed this for a while with awe, and then said, 'Sir, your face is turning red, your eyes are watering and you are choking. Why don't you stop eating these chillies?'

Nazrudin replied, 'I am waiting for a sweet one.'

We, too, are waiting for something, something that will sort out our financial woes. There must be something sweet at the bottom of the bag! However, the more you want and desire, the harder and more difficult your financial life becomes.

It's a very rewarding experience to check out what's cluttering up your financial life.

When you want to transform your finances and begin saving for the future, it goes without saying that you must create solid foundations. Although the idea of a budget or spending plan is often misunderstood, it is truly the foundation of any financial strategy.

As you work through the following questions in this chapter, you will be encouraged to reflect on your answers and work out ways to improve your current position. You may have to integrate some new, regular habits into your life. You may also decide to adopt a framework of professional advisers to support you.

This is, however, one area that you cannot delegate to someone else. The habits you form around cash and credit management have the potential to pay off for the rest of your life.

A simple system is to list all your direct debits, standing orders and regular financial commitments, *forget the numbers,* just the headings (mortgage, utility bills, mobile phone, children, charitable donations, insurance, savings, education, eating out, hairdresser, clothes, car loan, gym, hobbies etc.)

Now list these in order of priority, beginning with what you believe to be the most important. Then place the monetary cost against each and compare the amounts paid to those priority items with the more frivolous purchases.

Finally, ask yourself if you are happy with these findings? This reflects the earlier question of whether or not you are living your life in harmony with your basic values.

Although you may be tempted to charge ahead onto the following chapters, please do spend time thinking through all the practical steps you can take to reduce your outgoings, avoid those unnecessary treats, and make your cash work harder for you.

The following questions should be answered and scored regularly. Please record your score in **The WealthFlow System Scoring Table** and **Monthly Progress Chart**, which you'll find in the Appendix at the back of the book.

NOTE: Occasionally, you may honestly feel that a question is not relevant to your current situation. Simply award yourself 10 points. Be honest with yourself! Scoring 'Not Applicable' too often will only mislead you, and could draw you into a false sense of financial security.

Answer the following questions by ticking the appropriate box and calculating your score as follows:

10 points = Yes/Agree/Not Applicable
5 points = Not sure/Agree Sometimes
0 points = No/Disagree

QUESTIONS: **Breakthrough Cash & Credit Management**	**Answers** *(please tick)*	**Scoring**
p a s t		
1. Have you ever tracked all of your daily expenses for an entire month?	o Yes *(10)* o Not Sure *(5)* o No *(0)*	
2. Are you satisfied with the level of debt you have been carrying?	o Yes *(10)* o Not Sure *(5)* o No *(0)*	
3. Have you ever discussed your net worth and cash flow with a professional adviser?	o Yes *(10)* o Not Sure *(5)* o No *(0)*	
4. Do you know if your desired future lifestyle is financially achievable?	o Yes *(10)* o Not Sure *(5)* o No *(0)*	
5. Have you ever said 'No' when a bank or credit card company has offered to increase your credit limit?	o Yes *(10)* o Not Sure *(5)* o No *(0)*	
p r e s e n t		
6. Are you satisfied with the amount of money that you are able to spend on loved ones?	o Yes *(10)* o Not Sure *(5)* o No *(0)*	
7. Are you satisfied with your feelings towards money?	o Yes *(10)* o Not Sure *(5)* o No *(0)*	
8. Do you track your expenditure on a regular basis?	o Yes *(10)* o Not Sure *(5)* o No *(0)*	
9. Do you pay off credit card debt in full, on time, every month?	o Yes *(10)* o Not Sure *(5)* o No *(0)*	

10.	Do you have fewer than four credit and/or store cards?	o Yes *(10)* o Not Sure *(5)* o No *(0)*	
11.	Do you appreciate the merit in paying off debt, as opposed to simply investing excess capital?	o Yes *(10)* o Not Sure *(5)* o No *(0)*	
12.	Do you keep cash in a savings account and use only your current account to meet living expenses?	o Yes *(10)* o Not Sure *(5)* o No *(0)*	
13.	Do you move cash into a savings account before you buy those expensive treats each month?	o Yes *(10)* o Not Sure *(5)* o No *(0)*	
14.	Do you consciously avoid tapping into your overdraft on a regular basis?	o Yes *(10)* o Not Sure *(5)* o No *(0)*	
15.	Whenever necessary, is it easy for you to regularly lay your hands on specific credit card bills or bank statements?	o Yes *(10)* o Not Sure *(5)* o No *(0)*	
16.	Do you make and stick to a budget while you're on holiday?	o Yes *(10)* o Not Sure *(5)* o No *(0)*	
17.	Do you know the difference between an endowment mortgage and a repayment mortgage?	o Yes *(10)* o Not Sure *(5)* o No *(0)*	
18.	Do you pay all your bills on time?	o Yes *(10)* o Not Sure *(5)* o No *(0)*	
19.	Do you know the interest rate you are currently paying on your mortgage?	o Yes *(10)* o Not Sure *(5)* o No *(0)*	

	f u t u r e		
20.	Would you be happy to keep an honest diary of your daily expenses for one complete month?	o Yes *(10)* o Not Sure *(5)* o No *(0)*	
21.	Are you likely to set a budget for planned home improvements?	o Yes *(10)* o Not Sure *(5)* o No *(0)*	
22.	Are you satisfied with the level of service you receive from your bank/building society?	o Yes *(10)* o Not Sure *(5)* o No *(0)*	
23.	Are you satisfied with your ongoing levels of financial education?	o Yes *(10)* o Not Sure *(5)* o No *(0)*	
24.	Is it clear to you how you will pay off your mortgage and other debts in the future?	o Yes *(10)* o Not Sure *(5)* o No *(0)*	
25.	Do you keep a close eye on money that may be outstanding and due to you?	o Yes *(10)* o Not Sure *(5)* o No *(0)*	
26.	Are you satisfied with your ongoing ability to work within a budget?	o Yes *(10)* o Not Sure *(5)* o No *(0)*	
27.	Have you secured the best mortgage terms on your home(s)?	o Yes *(10)* o Not Sure *(5)* o No *(0)*	
28.	Have you enough money saved to support yourself for at least four months if you should lose your regular income (an emergency fund)?	o Yes *(10)* o Not Sure *(5)* o No *(0)*	
29.	Have you considered the merit of downsizing the family home at a future date?	o Yes *(10)* o Not Sure *(5)* o No *(0)*	

30.	Do you intend avoiding in-store cards when making major purchases?	o Yes *(10)* o Not Sure *(5)* o No *(0)*	
		WealthFlow System Score	**/ 300**
			%

TOTAL PERCENTAGE SCORED AND ITS SIGNIFICANCE	
85 – 100%	Your approach to Cash & Credit Management should meet your objectives
65 – 84%	Your approach to Cash & Credit Management needs more effort
Under 65%	Your approach to Cash & Credit Management needs to be reviewed

CASE STUDY

Avoiding The Debt Trap

'Credit card debt. I'm worried. I swore it wouldn't happen to me — but anyone who has children knows how hard it is to say 'No' to them. So when my youngest daughter asked for a new mountain bike and my teenage daughter asked for a laptop computer, as Christmas approached I was unable to avoid putting them on my card.

'Of course the problem now is that I'm dreading the day my credit card statement arrives in the post. My daughters' two expensive gifts, in addition to everyone else's presents, are going to burn a hole in my finances.

'So, in order to prepare for the inevitable bill, I contacted my professional adviser for help managing the credit card debt I accrued following my spending spree.

'She told me not to despair. By following a few simple guidelines, I could soon erase my Christmas debt and start the New Year on a more positive financial footing.

'First, she told me to stop incurring any new debt. By cutting out unnecessary spending and avoiding impulsive purchases, it would be easier to direct funds to where they are needed most — paying off my credit cards.

'Next, she advised me to avoid the financial black hole of accrued interest. Therefore, she suggested I pay as much off as I can every month while still leaving enough cash for vital expenses, such as food, transport and the mortgage.

'Third, I should consider using my investments to get out of debt. Although this initially seemed strange to me, she suggested I review the return being earned on my investments against the interest being charged on my debt. If the latter is higher, I should use my savings to rid myself of the debt and any interest that could be charged on that debt. After paying off the debt, any future earnings I would have applied to pay off the debt could be re-directed to new investments.

'Finally, my adviser stressed I should become more disciplined. Excessive spending can be a never-ending nightmare unless it is properly managed.'

Mrs DAC, London

PERSONAL COACHING TIPS

Ensure that you understand, perhaps with the help of your professional advisers, the following key areas:

- The major financial outgoings facing the family
- The major sources of income for the family
- The methods of releasing equity on property
- The common methods of mortgage loan repayments

Notes / Doodles

Personal Risk Management Programme | CHAPTER 03

> 'The woods are lovely, dark and deep. But I have promises to keep, and miles to go before I sleep.'
>
> ROBERT FROST
> 1875-1963, AMERICAN POET

Most people are confused about how much insurance and how much risk is appropriate. They wonder how an unexpected death, disability, or long-term care requirement would affect their family's security.

When Nazrudin's wife died, he didn't mourn for long. In fact, he seemed indifferent. However, a few months later, when his donkey died, he was very upset. He cried for days and lamented its loss. The villagers were curious.

'Dear sir,' one of them said, 'when your wife died, you didn't grieve at all. But your donkey's death shook you very deeply. You can't seem to get over it. What's the matter?'

'The night of my wife's funeral, all the neighbours, friends and relatives gathered in my house and said, "Don't worry, Nazrudin, we'll find you a younger, prettier bride; we'll wed you again; there are many good women out there; you won't be alone for long; we'll get you a better wife." Now my donkey is dead, but nobody is telling me that they will get me a younger, better donkey.'

When it comes to the subject of life insurance, I'm willing to bet that … *you don't really understand it … you may not like it … but you bought it anyway.*

The development of a life insurance plan begins with the question: *'Do you intend providing adequate support for someone when you die?'* This should also address the very real problem of being over-insured or having the wrong type of insurance. You may also wish to incorporate estate planning into an insurance philosophy, deciding whether beneficiaries should bear the costs of inheritance tax or whether the tax should be met from the proceeds of a life insurance policy — *see Chapter Seven: Estate Planning & Management Programme.*

Insurance is a thorny and difficult budgetary area to address. It adds insult to injury that we don't know whom to talk to about insurance except insurance salespeople. You should, however, seek help to guide you through the process of analysing your situation, determining your insurance needs, and buying the most suitable policies.

WHAT THE INSURANCE COMPANIES DON'T WANT YOU TO KNOW

The subject of life insurance often raises an element of scepticism; in my opinion, wrongly so. Surely, it cannot be the concept of insuring risk that makes us sceptical, so it must be the issue of commissions and whether or not we are being sold to or advised. If you have any concerns, these can be eliminated by paying your professional adviser a fee as opposed to the often confusing commission option. Astonishingly, the amount you pay for insurance products can often be reduced by as much as a third if commission is not taken.

The way it works is quite simple. The insurance company is effectively lending you the money to pay for advice. The company then increases the premium it charges to recoup the commission paid. Some companies make a considerable profit from this situation and are reluctant to see this approach come to an end.

Let us assume that you are paying £ 1,000 per month into a programme of savings and insurance products. Realistically, you could have the same investments, paying for them on a non-commission basis, for say £ 850. That would mean a regular saving of £ 150 per month, which adds up to £ 1,800 over the course of a year. Over a full 20 years, you would have saved £ 36,000.

If you have paid commission in the past, the most important thing is to ensure you don't pay it needlessly in the future.

Furthermore, it is sometimes possible to arrange for the removal of any additional ongoing contract charges associated with this 'commission loading'.

One day Nazrudin bought many goods at the market place and found a porter to carry all of his purchases. The porter had a large basket on his back and Nazrudin loaded everything he bought into the porter's basket. They headed towards Nazrudin's home, Nazrudin walking at the front and the porter following behind.

However, the dishonest porter preferred to make off with Nazrudin's purchases, rather than receiving a porter's fee. By the time Nazrudin noticed that the porter was no longer following him, the swindler had disappeared from sight. Nazrudin complained to his friends and neighbours but the porter was nowhere to be found.

Ten days later, as Nazrudin and his friends were sitting in the coffee house, someone spotted the thieving porter.

'Look, dear sir, isn't that the porter you lost?' Nazrudin's friend pointed to the man. But Nazrudin, instead of going up to the man and confronting him, tried to hide.

'Dear sir!' Everyone in the coffee house was surprised. 'Why don't you go and face the man?'

'What if,' Nazrudin said, 'he asks me to pay him ten days' worth of porter's fee?'

Knowing that death isn't just something that happens to other people is rarely reflected in a willingness to plan for the inevitable.

*'And come he slow, or come he fast,
It is but death who comes at last.'*

SIR WALTER SCOTT
1771-1832, SCOTTISH AUTHOR AND NOVELIST

The story goes that Nazrudin was called out to heal a rich landowner.

'Quick, give me a tonic to stop my stomach from splitting in two!'

'But what if the tonic fails to cure you?'

'How can it? You yourself once told me of its magic ingredients.'

'And what if I was mistaken?'

'Stop delaying. Without the medicine I will surely die.'

'With the medicine you will also die,' replied Nazrudin. 'It is just a matter of when and from what.'

'If my doctor told me I had only six minutes to live, I wouldn't brood. I'd type a little faster.'

ISAAC ASIMOV
1920-1992, WRITER OF OVER 500 BOOKS

This chapter recognises the acceptance and transfer of risk. In particular, catastrophes such as disability and the need for long-term care must be addressed. Why? Because these are areas which could destroy all of your goals and plans for the future. You could do well in every other area and still find yourself financially crippled.

The significant rise in long-term disability was once described to me as being a result of 'the airbag culture'. The description reflects our safety culture. Thanks to airbags, many people now survive potentially fatal situations, such as car accidents, when 15 years ago they would have been killed outright. This does not mean that accident victims just walk away from the scene. Rather, it means they go to Casualty instead of the mortuary.

So, if you think you will never suffer disability, or if you think it won't result in a financial burden, think again. Speak to your professional advisers about the main characteristics of the different types of income protection and long-term care insurance.

If you are in business, decide whether you want your business to outlive you. It is clear that no matter what type or size of business you have, you must think about its future and yours. It is prudent to consider the possibility of a business partner dying. It is also important to consider the possibility of a partner suffering a disability or illness that might keep him or her from working for many months or years.

> *'It is not in giving life but in risking life that man is raised above the animal.'*
>
> SIMONE DE BEAUVOIR
> 1908-1986, FRENCH FEMINIST WRITER

Let's assume for a moment that your life partner is gone; suddenly you're alone and life feels very numb. His or her death may have come as a complete shock or you may have been expecting it for a while.

Regardless of how it happened, the result will be the same. You are probably feeling very disconnected and sensing that this can't be real. Unfortunately, it is. You will, however, get through it and your days will get better again — but in the meantime, you have important tasks ahead of you.

You will be making a lot of decisions while in a vulnerable emotional state. The decisions you made beforehand now have real significance, as you deal with immediate as well as long-term financial issues.

Let's deal first with the immediate issues of funeral services. You'll need to get written estimates of what a funeral service will cost. Take some time in considering your options for a service. Do you want a traditional funeral, with or without viewing, with or without a graveside service? If you decide on cremation, will you have a memorial only? Will you have a ceremony for disposing of the ashes? What about a headstone? What kind do you want? What should it say?

An increasing number of people are uncomfortable with the idea of any kind of ceremony. All of the basic features of any funeral, including hymns and eulogies, are not what they want. For instance, a friend of mine has stated that his own preference would be for the remains to be disposed of quietly and without fuss — followed by a really good party with live music played by some of his musician friends.

> *'I'm not afraid to die, I just don't want to be there when it happens.'*
>
> WOODY ALLEN
> 1935- , AMERICAN FILM DIRECTOR AND COMEDIAN

It's important to avoid making assumptions about what you or your life partner really wants.

FUNERAL ARRANGEMENTS

Yourself		Your Life Partner	
Burial or cremation?		Burial or cremation?	
Preferred burial place/ash scattering?		Preferred burial place/ash scattering?	
Preferred inscription on memorial stone?		Preferred inscription on memorial stone?	
Preferred venue for funeral/memorial service?		Preferred venue for funeral/memorial service?	
Preferred person(s) to deliver address/eulogy?		Preferred person(s) to deliver address/eulogy?	
Preferred funeral director?		Preferred funeral director?	
Preferred pall bearers?		Preferred pall bearers?	
Preferred hymns/music?		Preferred hymns/music?	
List of people to be notified?		List of people to be notified?	
Other requests?		Other requests?	

You will need to check beneficiary designations on all life insurance policies.

Have the policies been set up correctly? It is not uncommon for a widow to find that her late husband forgot to change beneficiaries on remarrying, leaving insurance proceeds to an estranged first wife. Notify your loved one's present and all past employers (if they were working) and request a list of all benefits that are due. This may include unused sick time, a pension benefit, life insurance, and so on.

You need to compile a statement of net worth. Gather all investment statements and debt statements together. Put everything on it that you have knowledge of or suspect that you own. Compile information on your lifestyle costs — especially if you haven't been the person who was keeping track of them.

First, list all your fixed expenses and total them. This includes everything that is due each month, quarterly, or semi-annually. Next, list all your necessary living expenses and then the discretionary expenses that you wish to continue, assuming you wish to maintain a semblance of your current lifestyle. Remember, there is just one of you now — so some expenses will be less.

Even if you haven't been in the past, you must now become an excellent record keeper. Don't lose track of the good financial records that you are creating right now. Think about which financial strategies worked really well whilst your loved one was alive. You can start with a clean slate and create your own system. If you need help, an independent Certified Financial Planner (CFP) may be the right resource for you. *(Click on www.financialplanning.org.uk to find out more.)*

Don't rush to sell your home and move away from your familiar surroundings. Give it time. You may eventually do this — but let it be a decision that only came about after you did some advanced goal-setting. After twelve months, if you still want to move somewhere else, then you may be ready.

Don't even think of making loans to family members or friends. They may realise that you are coming into money through insurance proceeds (assuming these were arranged ahead of any illness) and more than one widow has been approached for familial loans at a time when they were generally too vulnerable to say no.

One good method for deflecting these requests is to cast a third party as the 'bad guy'. You can say that your financial planner, your accountant, the executor, or someone else must be consulted and that you must follow their recommendations. That will get you off the hook; generally speaking, the person asking for the money feels more uncomfortable once other people are likely to be involved.

Finally, do not make any investment decisions until at least six months have passed. During this time, keep your money safe and secure so that you don't have to worry about investment results (one less stress). Don't act on investment tips from family or friends. Lots of people will be willing to tell you what they have found to be good for them. That does not mean that it will be a good investment strategy for you.

Make sure you have the right financial planner *for you*: someone with the appropriate experience, someone compassionate and patient. Choose carefully. The integrity your planner brings to the process must be absolute and impeccable. At this point in your life, you may be vulnerable to money abuses. The last thing you need is a financial planner who also has financial reason and motivation to suggest acquisition of certain financial products. Seek a financial planner, preferably fee-based, who has no temptations that could colour any financial recommendations.

With your insurance issues taken care of, you are better protected against the financial consequences of a major misfortune and your family's security is strengthened.

Financial life planning is about helping you to take charge of your life. Don't ever think that someone else will take care of it for you. This attitude has led many people to remain uninformed, untrained, dependent, and unprepared for life changes. If you haven't done so already, take charge of your financial life before you find yourself alone.

'Most of us are anxious to improve our circumstances, but are unwilling to improve ourselves.'

JAMES ALLEN
1864-1912, WRITER

Whether you are facing a life changing event, such as the death of a loved one, or you simply want to take steps to improve your current situation, think of it as a crossroads where you can make many changes you never could before.

Start by re-reading the questions in *Chapter One: Progressive Life Planning & Management*, as well as the more specific questions at the end of this chapter. Spend lots of time with each question. Set aside plenty of time for this, so that you can decide what you really want. Create a vision of the results you want.

One way to do this is to think about what you want your life to look like, five years from now. What will you be doing? Where will you be living? What kind of friends will you have? What passions will fuel your day? How will you feel and look? What will you be wearing? What will your house look like? Allow yourself to fantasise about the perfect life in the perfect place. Write it down. Then start putting plans in place that allow you to work backwards from the vision to where you are now. This will help you develop the necessary actions that you need to take, to start moving towards that vision.

If you're ready to begin this next stage of your journey, you will probably feel a sense of excitement tinged with dread — along with a raft of other emotions. Everyone gets butterflies about now.

Approach it with an open mind. It is likely that you have gathered a great deal of life experience, and now is the time to look ahead and use that experience to best effect.

As you work through this next set of questions, you are again encouraged to reflect on your answers and work out ways to improve your current position. You will probably want to seek the support of a professional adviser.

Insuring unexpected risks is something that life assurance companies do well and I would encourage you against self-insuring, even if you have the capital resources to support yourself through disability or long-term care. Meeting these costs is simply not a good use of your hard-earned money. Ask your advisers for illustrations of cost and details of the various types of cover available.

The following questions should be answered and scored regularly. Please record your score in **The WealthFlow System Scoring Table** and **Monthly Progress Chart**, both of which are at the end of this book in the Appendix.

NOTE: If you honestly feel that a question is not relevant to your current situation, award yourself 10 points. Be honest with yourself! Scoring 'Not Applicable' too often will only mislead you, and draw you into a false sense of financial security.

Answer the following questions by ticking the appropriate box and calculating your score as follows:

10 points = Yes/Agree/Not Applicable
5 points = Not sure/Agree Sometimes
0 points = No/Disagree

QUESTIONS: **Personal Risk Management Programme**	**Answers** (*please tick*)	**Scoring**
p a s t		
1. Are you aware that past health issues might affect your ability to establish life insurance?	○ Yes *(10)* ○ Not Sure *(5)* ○ No *(0)*	
2. If asked, could you calculate the amount of money payable from existing life insurance policies on your death?	○ Yes *(10)* ○ Not Sure *(5)* ○ No *(0)*	
3. Are you comfortable with the methods used by your advisers to calculate exactly how much insurance cover is right for your personal circumstances?	○ Yes *(10)* ○ Not Sure *(5)* ○ No *(0)*	
4. Have your professional advisers fully explained the various ways of insuring personal risks?	○ Yes *(10)* ○ Not Sure *(5)* ○ No *(0)*	
5. Have you placed existing death policies in trust?	○ Yes *(10)* ○ Not Sure *(5)* ○ No *(0)*	
6. Are you aware of exactly how much ongoing commission is being earned by your advisers from your existing insurance policies?	○ Yes *(10)* ○ Not Sure *(5)* ○ No *(0)*	
p r e s e n t		
7. Do you understand the difference between *Critical Illness Cover* and *Permanent Health Insurance?*	○ Yes *(10)* ○ Not Sure *(5)* ○ No *(0)*	
8. Do you understand the difference between *Term Insurance* and *Whole of Life Assurance?*	○ Yes *(10)* ○ Not Sure *(5)* ○ No *(0)*	
9. Do you know where your insurance policies are stored and can you find them quickly?	○ Yes *(10)* ○ Not Sure *(5)* ○ No *(0)*	

10.	Have you established a cash reserve to support you/your family, immediately following death or disability?	o Yes *(10)* o Not Sure *(5)* o No *(0)*	
11.	Have you had your valuables assessed and valued recently for general insurance purposes (theft or damage)?	o Yes *(10)* o Not Sure *(5)* o No *(0)*	
12.	Are you satisfied with the level and quantity of life insurance protection you have?	o Yes *(10)* o Not Sure *(5)* o No *(0)*	
13.	If you are in business, have you protected the business from the loss of key personnel (death or disability, accident or sickness)?	o Yes *(10)* o Not Sure *(5)* o No *(0)*	
14.	If you are in business, have you established necessary buy/sell agreements, to enable the business to continue following your death or disability?	o Yes *(10)* o Not Sure *(5)* o No *(0)*	
15.	Have you read up on your current employer's in-house benefit schemes; death benefits, income protection and private medical insurance?	o Yes *(10)* o Not Sure *(5)* o No *(0)*	
16.	Have you considered the merits of private medical insurance for you and your family?	o Yes *(10)* o Not Sure *(5)* o No *(0)*	

f u t u r e

17.	Are you happy that your advisers are suitably qualified to advise you on life insurance contracts?	o Yes *(10)* o Not Sure *(5)* o No *(0)*	
18.	Have you considered the long-term inflationary impact on any existing 'fixed' sums assured, payable on death?	o Yes *(10)* o Not Sure *(5)* o No *(0)*	
19.	Do you know if the regular premiums you are paying for life insurance are competitive?	o Yes *(10)* o Not Sure *(5)* o No *(0)*	

20.	Have you thought through your funeral arrangements, and those of your partner?	o Yes *(10)* o Not Sure *(5)* o No *(0)*	
21.	In the event of a catastrophe, have you thought through the pros and cons of meeting your financial needs from your existing resources (capital and income) instead of buying insurance?	o Yes *(10)* o Not Sure *(5)* o No *(0)*	
22.	Have you considered life insurance as a means of passing on monies to charity?	o Yes *(10)* o Not Sure *(5)* o No *(0)*	
23.	Have you thought through the circumstances in which you would wish to downsize the family home?	o Yes *(10)* o Not Sure *(5)* o No *(0)*	
24.	Have you considered the need to insure the associated costs of long-term care?	o Yes *(10)* o Not Sure *(5)* o No *(0)*	
25.	Have you thought through what would happen if you no longer had a steady income and good health?	o Yes *(10)* o Not Sure *(5)* o No *(0)*	
		WealthFlow System Score	**/ 250**
			%

TOTAL PERCENTAGE SCORED AND ITS SIGNIFICANCE	
85 – 100%	Your approach to Personal Risk & Insurance Management should meet your objectives
65 – 84%	Your approach to Personal Risk & Insurance Management needs more effort
Under 65%	Your approach to Personal Risk & Insurance Management needs to be reviewed

CASE STUDY

Long-Term Care Insurance

'I clearly remember the day my mother was admitted to a residential nursing home. It was one of the most traumatic experiences of my life. After all, she made me the woman I am today.

'However, I was even more traumatised when I discovered the cost of her care. Naturally, I wanted to help her as much as I could, but I just wasn't able to, financially. And although my mother had a good career in the City, she was by no means a millionaire.

'After she died and we saw how much of her estate went to paying for care, my husband and I began to wonder about his parents and their ability to handle the costs of long-term care.

'That's when we contacted our professional adviser. She introduced us to long-term care insurance as the best way for my husband's parents to safeguard their assets, should their health become a concern.

'Thanks to my adviser's advice, we're resting a little easier now. My husband's parents' long-term care insurance policy will help ensure their quality of care — and more important their quality of life.'

Mrs ARB, Surrey

PERSONAL COACHING TIPS

Ensure that you understand, perhaps with the help of your professional advisers, the following key areas:

- The main types of term insurance and whole of life assurance, and their tax treatment
- The main types of health insurance cover
- The basic factors that need to be considered when choosing a protection product provider
- The merits of protecting yourself and your loved ones against all eventualities
- The main characteristics of the different types of long-term care products
- The effects and amounts of State benefits that may be available if you are in need of long-term care

Notes / Doodles

Savings, Investment and Risk Integration | CHAPTER 04

> 'Sometimes your best investments are the ones you don't make.'
>
> DONALD TRUMP
> 1946- , AMERICAN BUSINESSMAN

The recent underperformance of stock markets has caused a lot of rethinking about how to invest money.

The one definitive conclusion is that simply trying to maximise return is no longer adequate. Managing for maximum return ignores the fact that you may be able to afford less risk and still meet your goals.

> *The story goes that Nazrudin was asleep and dreaming when a hand reached out of nowhere and dropped a gold coin in front of him. Again and again, the hand let coins fall until they numbered ninety-nine. Just as the hand was coming forth with the hundredth coin, it began to fade. Before the last piece of gold fell, the hand completely disappeared.*
>
> *'No, no! I want one hundred!' Nazrudin screamed, so loudly that he awakened himself and sat up in the bed.*
>
> *The ever-canny Nazrudin lay back down, pulled the pillow over his eyes, and said softly, 'Okay, okay. I'll take ninety-nine.'*

All too often, we desire that elusive additional return — but at what risk?

The real issue is matching your future assets with your future liabilities. For example, you may want to reduce your working hours at a certain age, and fund your children's education at a certain time, or generally need specific amounts of cash at predictable times in the future. Financial life planning is about helping you achieve your goals, not simply about attaining the highest investment return.

Perhaps the key part of financial life planning is the integrated approach to looking after your financial affairs; being able to see the broader picture. As a result of gathering the widest possible range of information — on matters ranging from lifestyle choices to housing needs, from pension provision to educational ambitions for children and grandchildren — you are given a greater insight into your total asset position than is the case with traditional financial advice. The life planning questions posed in *Chapter One: Progressive Life Planning & Management* and the chapter-specific questions testify to that.

Remember, there is no quick fix. It is not about chasing the next hot investment fund or what is fashionable (for example, technology, football or telecommunication stocks, or buy-to-let residential properties). Typically, get-rich-quick schemes are developed to entrap the weak and especially the poor.

After all, what does a wealthy person need with a get-rich-quick scheme?

Financial education is often limited to what we hear or see on television. In my experience this is usually worthless. It's equivalent to horse-racing pundits filling in the gaps between races with tips and guesswork.

In August 2001, I read an article that strengthened these views. It was written by Bob Veres, the leading US commentator on the future of the financial planning profession. It was entitled, Talk Show Investing. He argued that 'nobody ever gives the financial planning perspective on television'. 'What is preached is too often hot tips rather than sensible diversification or protection against falling markets'. He went on to explain that these hot tips could not be further from the financial planning perspective on investing.

The internet has, of course, increased the problem because unsophisticated investors, with money they often cannot afford to lose, are buying and selling stocks and shares — in other words, *day trading*.

I have a friend who traded Penny Shares and thought it great that he was making money. What he didn't know was the cost of trading (around 10%), the investment risks or indeed anything about the companies he invested in. He subsequently lost the lot.

Equally, listening to someone spouting forth on breakfast television news is not the way to a secure financial future. Bob Veres points out that their message is fundamentally flawed, since they imply that you can 'beat the market if only you can get sufficient up-to-the-minute information'.

The financial planning assumption, on the other hand, is that the only sure way to make money in the markets is to select investments with at least a five year holding period in mind — and preferably 10, 20, or more!

Word got out that Nazrudin possessed a jar full of vinegar that was 40 years old. One day a neighbour came knocking on the door.

'Dear sir, is it really true that you have a jar full of 40-year-old vinegar?'

'It is true,' Nazrudin replied.

'Could I have a cupful of that vinegar?'

'No,' said Nazrudin tersely.

'But, dear sir,' the displeased neighbour pursued, 'why won't you give me some? I only asked for a cupful.'

'Because,' Nazrudin explained, 'if I were to give a cupful to everyone who asked, my vinegar wouldn't have lasted for 40 years.'

'Our favourite holding period is forever.'

WARREN BUFFETT
1930- , AMERICAN INVESTMENT ENTREPRENEUR

Now that you know a little more about the financial life planning way of looking at things, see if you can imagine a financial life planner's response to the usual financial and business media coverage that we tend to see on television and in the press.

Bob Veres' article, based upon a scripted interview, paints the picture of a financial expert sitting in a smart suit, the interviewer leaning forward for the first question. The atmosphere is polite and even humorous.

From a UK perspective the interview would probably begin: 'Where do you think interest rates are going to be in the next couple of weeks? What do you think of the nation's favourite high street store's latest attempt at recovery? Can you tell us where you see the Footsie 100 in three-to-six-months' time?'

FTSE Index ('Footsie 100') — Financial Times Stock Exchange Share Index. The index plots the share price value of the 100 largest companies listed on the London Stock Exchange.

The truth is, any financial life planner worth his salt knows that this sort of chatter is all hogwash. It is similar to the media's fascination with telling us the level of the 'Footsie 100' every evening. And as highlighted by Bob Veres in the US, the same misguided nonsense is talked the world over.

Does anyone really care about those questions? Have you ever caught yourself thinking: 'Wow, the market's sitting at 4831 today, and last night it was around 4901!'

Bob Veres believes that a financial planner's natural response to those out of context numbers would be: 'So what? It's completely irrelevant to serious investing.' And I agree with him.

Worse still, I cannot remember a single occasion when anyone from any media channel explained to the viewers what the Footsie represents, when it began, how often the companies within the Index change, and whether it is weighted or unweighted.

All we get is the 'number'.

No one can foretell the future. Most financial planners accepted this a long time ago. What about Government gilts, or National Savings, or how best to hold cash on deposit, or the benefits of reducing your debt? These subjects are rarely addressed on television because they are not as sexy as having a go at guessing the next big thing.

Bob Veres highlights the real revelation: investing was never meant to be sexy or exciting. 'Any exciting thing you do with your portfolio will probably be harmful to your future financial health.' I agree. I'm talking from painful experience.

Finally, Bob issues a word of warning. Remember this: any hot tips that imply knowledge that the rest of the market doesn't have would mean 'valuable inside information'. The broker-tipster must notify the market and is prohibited from encouraging others to trade. Does this mean that the nice man on the breakfast television show could be breaking the law, that he's a criminal? Hopefully, he is simply 'pretending to have inside information' and therefore his only crime is to lie to the watching viewers, a few million people.

Few tipsters are ever invited back to comment on their predictions. It would, in any case, be difficult because the return might take years to materialise. Will you remember? Will you care?

> **Active investment — where the investor attempts to beat the performance of the market.**
> **Passive investment — where a representative portfolio of shares is carefully selected and then left untouched until the money is needed.**

Many active investment managers attempt to outperform the market, using the basic argument that even an additional return of 1%, particularly when it's 1% compounded year after year, can represent a lot of money. Some of these managers might even be right to take the additional risks in their attempts to outperform the market. This is for you to decide, based on your own experiences and current professional relationships.

However, 'over-emphasising' investment returns in order to impress, perhaps to win you over, has gone on for many years and will I'm sure go on for many more.

> *Two Persians were passing through the village. Nazrudin and other villagers were chatting with them in the coffee house. One of the Persians was talking endlessly about the splendours and prosperity of Persia.*
>
> *'In our city Esfahan, the Shah has a palace that is 5,000 yards in length and has 200 rooms.' He was going on and on. Nazrudin wanted to reciprocate with some boasting of his own.*

> *'Our city Bursa has even bigger palaces. And furthermore, there is a new spa built around the thermal springs. It is 10,000 yards in length and...'*

> *'I know Bursa very well,' the other Persian interrupted. Upon hearing this, Nazrudin wanted to cut his tall tale short.*

> *'And it is 50 yards in width,' he concluded sheepishly. Nazrudin's friends noticed the disparity between the proportions.*

> *'Dear sir,' they whispered, 'the width doesn't go with the length.'*

> *'Had this man not claimed to know Bursa well,' Nazrudin replied, 'I was going to match the width to the length.'*

> *'Investment managers and their clients would be wise to devote more attention to understanding the real advantages offered by the market fund (index-tracker) — the powerful plodder.'*
>
> CHARLES D ELLIS
> AUTHOR OF INVESTMENT POLICY: HOW TO WIN THE LOSER'S GAME

You are probably fooling yourself if you think you can beat the market. Of course, many people like to manage their own investments — they like the challenge of trying to beat the market — but it is not necessarily profitable. Generally speaking, over the long-term and after costs, passive investment is better than active investment. The ideal investment strategy has two golden rules: diversify as much as possible; and transact (buy/sell) as little as possible.

> *'It is difficult to understand why the world is full of active investors.'*
>
> PROFESSOR S M KEANE MS LLB PhD GLASGOW CA
> HEAD OF ACCOUNTING AND FINANCE, GLASGOW UNIVERSITY

It should come as little surprise that active investment managers, who account for the bulk of the market, have a hard time beating their own kind. An analysis of historical data makes it hard to support the conclusion that active managers as a group can generate significant added value. This suggests that believing in active management is more akin to an act of faith than a sound financial philosophy.

After many years of advocating active investment management, I became enlightened to the fact that passive investment (or 'indexing') does very well. Index funds try to capture the returns of a particular stock market index, by buying a representative portion of the equities in that index.

You could throw darts at the *Financial Times* pages and do better than most active managers. The simple problem is the management costs! The higher-cost funds are typically those associated with active management. The reality is that we are headed for a lower-return environment where most of the sexier funds will disappoint their investors. In these circumstances, the best thing an investor can do is control expenses and be realistic on expectations.

As reported in the May 2004 edition of *financialalert* (New Zealand), Burton Malkiel, author of *A Random Walk Down Wall Street* is reported to have said: 'If I went out on my local golf course and shot par, I'd be pleased with myself. If I knew I could shoot par on every round, I'd consider myself a good golfer. However, when it comes to investing money, for some reason, when people are offered a par score on their investments, they think it's boring — even when, long-term, they beat 90% of the actively-managed alternatives.'

Perhaps the most important lesson of all is learning how best to spread your money around. Known as 'asset allocation', this is all about positioning assets within a portfolio to maximise return for a given risk tolerance. The principle behind asset allocation is rather simple. Based on Nobel Prize-winning research, the theory is that the more classes of assets used to make up a portfolio, the lower the volatility (risk).

Put simply, clients who can afford to take more risk — they are said to have *high risk tolerance* — should expect to see more of their money invested in aggressive investment classes (tamed a little when combined with other asset classes). Very conservative clients, on the other hand, with a lower risk tolerance, will lean towards cash, 'blue chip' equities and highly-rated corporate and Government bonds.

This is not to say that picking a great asset allocation model compensates for picking lousy investments. Nothing could be further from the truth. In fact, you must carefully allocate your assets, and then select the proper investments for each allocation. Detailed analysis of historical performance is critical to this equation, and your advisers should ensure that you are fully involved in this process in order to minimise the risk of any misunderstandings.

The original award-winning study of pension plans found that 93.6% of the difference in performance from one plan to another was due to asset allocation, not individual investment selection. Thus, investors who devote all their time to considering which shares to buy are missing the point — as are the magazines, television show investment pundits and newsletters that proclaim with each issue: *'This Month's Hot Share Tips!'*

> *'Risk comes from not knowing what you're doing.'*
>
> WARREN BUFFETT

For clients in retirement, who require an income-generating portfolio of investments, my own preference is to allow asset allocation to be driven by their future cash flow needs:

1. Calculate your following year's income requirement
2. Hold a suitable cash reserve representing two-years' worth of your income needs
3. Keep an additional rolling three-years' worth of income in low risk bonds
4. Invest the remaining assets in accordance with whichever asset allocation is most likely to achieve the necessary rate of return in order to meet your pre-agreed goals

Once a year you would sell enough long-term assets to top up the cash reserve to meet the following year's income requirement, and so on. This effectively provides five-years' worth of living expenses at hand. It is something with which clients feel very comfortable.

Such decisions should only be made after a comprehensive review of your present financial situation has been undertaken, establishing your goals and priorities as well as the pros and cons of various investment options.

A major flaw in traditional financial services is the avoidance of truly searching questions which would allow a clearer understanding of your financial needs. Instead, there is a preference for taking all the money you have available, and agreeing a level of risk based on scant information, with a view to maximising returns.

In December 2003, the Financial Services Authority (FSA) fined one of the UK's leading personal financial services companies a total of £ 2,320,000 for serious compliance failings; part of which stemmed from insufficient *know your customer* requirements, a basic tenet of financial planning advice.

The Certified Financial Planning (CFP) Board defines the financial planning process in part as *'gathering client data including goals'* and *'analysing and evaluating the client's financial status'*. These two activities are considered to be critical to financial planning. However, many advisers continue to practise only a narrow subset of financial planning — namely **investment planning**.

FINANCIAL PLANNING DEFINED

Comprehensive financial planning is the process of determining how best to meet your goals through close management of financial resources.

The outcome is objective and includes:

Comprehensive Financial Planning	The WealthFlow System
1. Financial budgeting and planning	• Breakthrough Cash & Credit Management
2. Risk management	• Personal Risk Management Programme
3. Investment planning	• Savings, Investment & Risk Integration
4. Retirement planning	• Retirement & Life Transition Management
5. Income tax planning	• Tax Planning & Mitigation Programme
6. Estate planning	• Estate Planning & Management Programme

Financial planners offer intellectual capital and advice — as opposed to simple product selection. Indeed, product selection and implementation may or may not be done by the financial planner.

As referred to earlier, managing money simply to maximise investment return ignores the fact that you may be able to afford less risk, with more consistency, and still meet your goals.

If you cannot achieve your goals based on realistic rates of return — amend your goals!

Finally, should you stay loyal to the original asset allocation model?

This is often referred to as rebalancing. Rebalancing means that you react to one asset class growing and another shrinking by acting to maintain your original asset allocation percentages. The good news is that this forces you to sell high (the asset that has risen most in value thereby causing the imbalance) and buy low (the asset that is out of favour and cheaper at this time).

This addresses the most fundamental issues — when to sell a strongly performing asset class and when to sell an underperformer. It is all too easy to hold on to both: the high performer hoping it will rise further, and the poor performer hoping for recovery.

At the very least, rebalancing creates the discipline to sell and buy that is typically missing in do-it-yourself portfolio management. Think of the rising markets of the late 1990s. Yes, rebalancing would have curtailed your gains — but when the crashes came, rebalancing would have put you in much better shape and curtailed your losses. Like most strategies, you shouldn't become a slave to the original asset allocation model.

As your situation changes you should revisit the original asset allocation decision. An aggressive portfolio may have seemed perfect in the late 1990s, but by 2004 you may well have grown more risk averse, having experienced volatile and uncertain markets. You will, of course, be closer to your original goal, which may naturally lead you to take a more conservative approach as the goal comes closer into view.

In other words, asset allocating and rebalancing is a continuous process requiring you to sell your winning asset classes (the ones that made you the most money) and buy your losing asset classes (the ones that made the least money, or perhaps even lost money).

You may think this is crazy, but think about it: if your professional advisers spend their time *selling winners* and *buying losers*, you will become very, very wealthy.

Why don't you want to buy winners? Because, generally speaking, they have already made their money. All that matters is that it became a winner *before you sold it*.

As an investor, the following gems may prove useful in thinking through future decisions:

1. If you must play the market, don't speculate to satisfy some emotional need. Recognise this behaviour as gambling — and, if you dare, keep accurate records so you can quantify your losses!

2. Avoid the media and their tipsters.

3. Remember, most tax shelters are high risk. The reason you're allowed to shelter tax at all is simply to encourage you to invest — often in things you would otherwise avoid.

4. Be wary of treating your home as an investment. Although the last 20 years have been good for house prices, the future may be very different as the control of land by Britain's elite comes under increased pressure to be released for house building. The power of supply and demand is at work, but this may not last. The UK is not short of land on which to build houses.

5. Never invest in anything you don't understand or which cannot be clearly explained to you. Over the last 15 years all of the financial services industry's mis-selling has evolved around complex products which neither adviser nor client truly understood. Greed won the day.

6. Be alert to how stockbrokers work. If a stockbroker manages £ 10 million, to earn his £ 100,000 salary, he must typically generate £ 300,000 in gross commission — that's 3% of the money. If the stockbroker is advising 250-300 clients, he does not have time to learn what is best. He just needs to keep your money turning, earning commissions on every piece of 'advice'.

7. Don't invest in off-the-page newspaper launches. They have no track record and often have more marketing than investment substance. The patients have taken over the asylum, with most marketing departments controlling investment management houses. The reason? New fund launches draw new money (or churned old money), the life blood of the investment industry.

8. Write out your short-medium and long-term goals and stick with them. *Plan* your success.

9. Don't forget about inflation. The Rule of 72 is a simple method of calculating the approximate number of periods over which a quantity will halve in value. If you were to leave £ 10,000 uninvested when inflation was 9% per annum, the purchasing power of your £ 10,000 would have halved after eight years (72/9). So, think about retiring with capital that must last 30 years.

10. The most financially successful people tend to save at least 20% of their income. Attempting this level of saving may be too radical for you at the moment, but do something now, even if the step you take is a small one. Your financial situation says a lot more about you than your money. If you want to live a truly fulfilled life, taking charge of your savings is crucial.

Once you feel more comfortable over your ability to make better investment decisions, you'll feel more inspired to control your future. The more confident you feel about your future the more easily you'll find it coming to life. The time you spend taking an interest in how your money is invested will prove invaluable in shaping your destiny.

The following questions will help you reflect on your own savings and investment options. This is an important part of financial life planning. It's inspiring to look to your future, creating the opportunity to focus on what's truly important to you.

Please record your score in **The WealthFlow System Scoring Table** and **Monthly Progress Chart** in the Appendix.

NOTE: If you honestly feel that a question is not relevant to your current situation, award yourself 10 points. Be honest with yourself! Scoring 'Not Applicable' too often will only mislead you, and draw you into a false sense of financial security.

Answer the following questions by ticking the appropriate box and calculating your score as follows:

10 points = Yes/Agree/Not Applicable
5 points = Not sure/Agree Sometimes
0 points = No/Disagree

QUESTIONS: **Savings, Investment and Risk Integration**	**Answers** *(please tick)*	**Scoring**
p a s t		
1. Are you aware of how your investments have performed over the past five years?	o Yes *(10)* o Not Sure *(5)* o No *(0)*	
2. Have you defined your attitude towards investment risk and the level of risk you are comfortable with?	o Yes *(10)* o Not Sure *(5)* o No *(0)*	
3. Have you been saving at least 10% of your income on a regular basis?	o Yes *(10)* o Not Sure *(5)* o No *(0)*	
4. Are you aware of how much commission your advisers have earned from advising you?	o Yes *(10)* o Not Sure *(5)* o No *(0)*	
5. Have previous advisers explained the importance of *asset allocation* when making investment decisions?	o Yes *(10)* o Not Sure *(5)* o No *(0)*	
6. Do you understand the tax advantages of unit trusts/investment trusts over owning individual shareholdings (equities)?	o Yes *(10)* o Not Sure *(5)* o No *(0)*	
7. Do you know how much risk and volatility is present in your existing portfolio of savings and investments?	o Yes *(10)* o Not Sure *(5)* o No *(0)*	
8. Could you lower your portfolio's risk profile and still achieve your investment goals?	o Yes *(10)* o Not Sure *(5)* o No *(0)*	
9. Have you enquired about the choice of investments held within your employer's pension scheme?	o Yes *(10)* o Not Sure *(5)* o No *(0)*	
10. Have you ever set yourself an annual savings target and stuck to it?	o Yes *(10)* o Not Sure *(5)* o No *(0)*	

		present	
11.	Do you understand the importance of *diversification*?	o Yes *(10)* o Not Sure *(5)* o No *(0)*	
12.	Do you save so much that you feel a little 'squeezed' each month?	o Yes *(10)* o Not Sure *(5)* o No *(0)*	
13.	Do you have more money in savings than you owe on your credit cards?	o Yes *(10)* o Not Sure *(5)* o No *(0)*	
14.	Are you able to save regularly, ahead of paying the bills?	o Yes *(10)* o Not Sure *(5)* o No *(0)*	
15.	Are you clear about the differences between *investing* and *gambling*?	o Yes *(10)* o Not Sure *(5)* o No *(0)*	
16.	Are you happy with the amount you spend on your children/close family?	o Yes *(10)* o Not Sure *(5)* o No *(0)*	
17.	Do you sleep at night, knowing that your investments are well planned?	o Yes *(10)* o Not Sure *(5)* o No *(0)*	
18.	Are you happy with your existing investment advisers?	o Yes *(10)* o Not Sure *(5)* o No *(0)*	
19.	Are you totally honest with yourself about your money situation?	o Yes *(10)* o Not Sure *(5)* o No *(0)*	
		future	
20.	Do you have an opinion on the long-term effects of inflation?	o Yes *(10)* o Not Sure *(5)* o No *(0)*	

No.	Question	Options	Score
21.	Do you intend saving regularly from income?	o Yes *(10)* o Not Sure *(5)* o No *(0)*	
22.	Do you accept that you cannot consistently outsmart the investment markets?	o Yes *(10)* o Not Sure *(5)* o No *(0)*	
23.	Do you accept the significant long-term benefit of re-investing dividends?	o Yes *(10)* o Not Sure *(5)* o No *(0)*	
24.	Do you accept that you cannot consistently time the market, sell at its peak and buy when it hits bottom?	o Yes *(10)* o Not Sure *(5)* o No *(0)*	
25.	Do you accept that your investments will not simply look after themselves?	o Yes *(10)* o Not Sure *(5)* o No *(0)*	
26.	Do you appreciate that there are times when you should sell an investment that has lost money?	o Yes *(10)* o Not Sure *(5)* o No *(0)*	
27.	Do you have people (friends/advisers) around you who will support you with your financial plans?	o Yes *(10)* o Not Sure *(5)* o No *(0)*	
28.	Do you appreciate that investment selection based on strict ethical and/or environmental criteria will limit your investment options?	o Yes *(10)* o Not Sure *(5)* o No *(0)*	
29.	Do you understand the importance of *rebalancing* your investment portfolio?	o Yes *(10)* o Not Sure *(5)* o No *(0)*	
30.	Do you have clear ideas of how you want your money to work for you?	o Yes *(10)* o Not Sure *(5)* o No *(0)*	
		WealthFlow System Score	/ 300
			%

TOTAL PERCENTAGE SCORED AND ITS SIGNIFICANCE	
85 – 100%	Your approach to Savings, Investment & Risk Integration should meet your objectives
65 – 84%	Your approach to Savings, Investment & Risk Integration needs more effort
Under 65%	Your approach to Savings, Investment & Risk Integration needs to be reviewed

CASE STUDY

Asset Management: Coping With Difficult Financial Times

'I've always been an independent person. I prefer being responsible for my actions — both good and bad. That's why I thoroughly enjoy the game of chess. It's just me and my opponent — one on one.

'Unfortunately, I've always approached my finances with much the same mentality. I enjoy the intellectual stimulation of making investment decisions myself. However, recent stock market volatility has made that more difficult.

'So, I decided to call my brother's financial planner for help. Although I thought I was doing well before the market's latest downturn, she reviewed my portfolio and informed me otherwise. She said I had very low cash reserves, highly-geared investments and little diversification. All told, my investment portfolio was rather poorly.

'I've learnt that diversification plays a large part in long-term success. Spreading assets across a variety of different investments (asset classes) is perhaps the single most important rule I've learnt as an investor. Each kind of investment follows a cycle of its own and each responds differently to changes in the economy.

'So, by owning a variety of assets, declines in some of my investments have been balanced by stability — and, sometimes, increased value — in another. All of this helps me on my way to my long-term financial goals… what's really important.

'That's why I decided to delegate all of the day-to-day decisions — such as which unit trusts or investment trusts to hold and when to buy or sell — to professionals who focus their full-time attention on asset allocation and fund selection, and who seek to maximise the returns my assets can bring.

'Thanks to the relationship I've established with my financial planner, I have a level of financial confidence I have never known before. And now, when the market takes an unexpected turn, I'm no longer concerned with how to fix my portfolio — improving my chess game comes first.'

Mr SSP, Edinburgh

PERSONAL COACHING TIPS

Ensure that you understand, perhaps with the help of your professional advisers, the following key areas:

- The assumptions being made in respect of inflation and rates of return
- The impact of investment risk and the various levels
- The common investment products in terms of risk
- The importance of asset allocation
- The importance of investment *tax wrappers* such as Personal Equity Plans, Individual Savings Accounts, Self Invested Personal Pensions, personal pensions, offshore investments and charitable trusts
- The major characteristics of bank, building society and National Savings products
- The major characteristics of *securities* (gilts, corporate bonds and equities)
- The major characteristics of *packaged investments* such as unit trusts, life policies and investment trusts savings schemes
- The tax treatment of packaged investments
- Why packaged investments can frequently suit your needs and circumstances

Notes / Doodles

Retirement and Life Transition Management | CHAPTER 05

> *'A person can stand almost anything except a succession of ordinary days.'*
>
> JOHANN WOLFGANG VON GOETHE
> 1749-1832, GERMAN WRITER, SCIENTIST AND PHILOSOPHER

Many of us have real concerns about life's transitions. These are not just financial — indeed, the financial situation can be quantified — it is the other, more personal, aspects that are likely to be the real cause of anxiety. But just like anything we strive for, the quest for financial security in later life can blind us to life's other worthy goals and remove us from the present moment.

You need look no further than the best-seller lists to witness our growing concerns over retirement and money ... *Rich Dad's Retire Young Retire Rich; Retire Worry-free; Retire Right; Retire and Thrive; The Millionaire Next Door; Think and Grow Rich; The Courage to be Rich.* Quite obviously, when many people think of happiness and success, the first thing they envision is having plenty of money.

I have long been an advocate of controlling personal expenditure. I have seen for myself how clients with ordinary incomes could potentially accumulate enough to provide financial freedom, whilst those on far greater incomes struggled. My own experience of taking a career break to write this book and plan a new business has strengthened this belief, setting myself the goal of living off a tight budget.

> *In another Nazrudin story, a mother asks Nazrudin, who is this time a judge, to forbid her son to eat more than a certain amount of sugar each day, explaining that Nazrudin must do this because the boy won't obey her. Nazrudin asks her to come back in a week.*
>
> *She does, and he then asks her to come back in another week. Again, she does. This time he forbids the boy to eat more than a certain quantity of sugar each day.*
>
> *The mother then asks him why it took him so long to make such a simple order. And Nazrudin replies that because he was a sugar eater when she first came to him, he first had to see if he could get by on so little sugar, before he could ask anyone else to do it.*

This is not just a joke, as it might appear at first glance, but an illustration of Sufi principles — that you can only truly teach that which you truly know. Instead of relying on the old parental adage: *'Do as I say, not as I do,'* Sufis are only called to ask for conduct which is consistent with their own.

The goal for most people must be to cut expenses to a level that can potentially be supported by investments. Simple!

Not so simple in fact, but a good start in planning our futures. Prove it to yourself. Take a look at your income and expenditure patterns and clarify where the money goes. Look at ways in which you can reduce your monthly expenditure by 10-30%.

As stated in *Chapter Two: Breakthrough Cash & Credit Management*, it's not how much you earn that determines your financial situation, but how much you keep!

The results of our excesses are all around us. A close friend in New York tells me of £ 190,000 bar mitzvahs in Manhattan and gifts of kiddie-sized fully operational Porsche Carreras (£ 15,000) — gifts for children.

Re-read *Chapter Two*. As homework, I challenge you to team up with your partner or a close friend to go through your own expenditure and see where you can cut back. Why not set a goal of reducing your outgoings by 25%? Begin by listing at least five things you can start doing to reduce your expenditure.

Often the largest money saver is to remortgage at a more competitive interest rate; a 1% reduction in mortgage rate based on a £ 100,000 interest-only mortgage will save you £ 1,000 in year one. If you are a higher rate taxpayer and invest this saving into a pension, you will receive tax breaks equating to another £ 400. Remember — in order to pay that extra £ 1,000 a year in mortgage interest you have had to earn in excess of £ 1,400 before tax (income tax and National Insurance).

Once you've done this exercise, find 12 unrewarding ways that you currently spend your money. (Gadgets, taxis and parking fines were collectively my own Achilles heel.)

> *'Annual income twenty pounds, annual expenditure nineteen pounds nineteen and six, result happiness. Annual income twenty pounds, annual expenditure twenty pounds nought and six, result misery.'*
>
> SAID BY MR MICAWBER IN DAVID COPPERFIELD BY CHARLES DICKENS

Bearing in mind that retirement planning is often the primary reason people go to financial planners, let me begin by introducing you to Anna and Louise, neighbours of mine.

Anna and Louise were friends. Anna had retired from a successful family business at the age of 50, while Louise was forced to work on as she believed she had not built up sufficient funds to support herself. Anna was able to move to the south of France. Louise remained in Scotland wishing she had planned a little earlier for the future – birthday and Christmas email messages were exchanged in an effort to keep in touch.

A school reunion finally created the opportunity to meet up, some five years or so later. It was at this time that Anna confided in Louise that she was very lonely – she felt forgotten. Very few of her old friends even knew she had moved to France.

Anna was confused, she had worked so hard in the family business and always thought that retirement was her prize for forging a successful career, all those late nights in the office and weekends given up, for what? For this?

The situation will no doubt strike a chord with you through personal experience of others, perhaps even family members.

It was around this time that a friend gave me a copy of a book entitled *The New Retirementality* (Dearborn Trade). Author Mitch Anthony talks about a similar example, this time, two men separated by retirement. One of these men believed he had reached a finishing line in his life – *the institution of retirement*. Once he reached it, he didn't know where to go. Anthony talks about the feelings of boredom and dejection.

'Before deciding to retire early, take a fortnight off and watch daytime television.'

ANONYMOUS

Retirement generally is based upon the belief that you work until somewhere between 60 and 65. This belief is centred upon an outdated perception of what retirement involves. A generation or more later, Governments are now faced with the dilemma of a costly social system, and the growing recognition that for many of us some form of paid employment beyond age 65 is needed. This may be a result of financial need. Other people simply wish to remain within the game and benefit from its many challenges.

When age 65 was originally set as the State retirement age in the UK, the Government of the day anticipated very little time between retirement and death. Now, align that thought with today's expectation that retirement should last 20, 30 or even 40 years. The significant improvements in lifestyle and life expectancy have also resulted in serious worries over employer-funded pension arrangements — specifically, the costs of providing pensions over such a long timescale and reliance on healthy stock market returns.

The New Retirementality paints a picture of traditional retirement, reflecting the fact that retirement was seen as an opportunity to live a little. From an employer's perspective the ability to retire an older worker and replace him or her with a sprightly 20 year old was often much more productive. That, of course, is no longer true. Today we trade intellect and know-how. The 60 year old's knowledge of how to get things done has often become invaluable.

Mitch Anthony relates: 'Society made retirement a time of extraction, the date when you moved to the periphery.'

It sent out detrimental messages that you no longer mattered. It was obvious that this mindset had to change.

The experiences of Anna and Louise may prompt you to re-examine your thoughts on traditional retirement. In doing so, you need to acknowledge that work brings with it many unpaid benefits — benefits which you might find hard to give up.

> *'Nothing is really work unless you would rather be doing something else.'*
>
> JAMES M BARRIE
> 1860-1937, SCOTTISH DRAMATIST AND NOVELIST

Studies show that the majority of retirees are now re-engaging in some sort of work, either part time or full time. Mitch Anthony says: 'Work is no longer the enemy. A perhaps unsurprising side effect is that many couples begin to suffer marital stresses when one or both parties retire. The marriage relationship only returns to normality when one or both parties go back to work.'

> *Nazrudin's wife died. When friends and relatives came to console him, they found him quite indifferent. As they tried to say a few comforting words, Nazrudin interrupted them.*
>
> *'Don't worry,' he said, 'even if she hadn't died, I was going to divorce her anyway.'*

You or your parents may have already been exposed to traditional retirement planning, treated as purely a financial deadline. An example is the financial adviser who simply reviews how much money you have before informing you that you can or cannot retire.

Traditional retirement planning brings many traumas, whereas financial life planning develops a different set of rules, about setting goals and uncovering dreams.

Mitch Anthony concludes: 'It's often not about the money. It's about alienation, being cut off from the people and the processes and the projects that used to make you excited and feel part of something bigger than yourself. Feelings of alienation are closely followed by boredom and detachment and potentially the loss of self-esteem. This can mean the move from being a *Who's Who* to Who's He? For others it is the frustration of no longer being the person you were and the perception of others that you are just another retiree.'

> *'What the caterpillar calls the end of the world, others call a butterfly.'*
>
> ANONYMOUS

The truth is, we're not designed for full time leisure. It is probably fair to say that full retirement for most people is simply a dangerous illusion. Leisure time is wonderful when you can fit it in, but a horrible choice for everyday living.

I take inspiration from Roy R Neuberger, founder of the investment management firm Neuberger Berman. He is a renowned professional investor, and recognised collector of American art of his time. From its founding in 1939, Neuberger Berman focused on managing money for wealthy individuals. Mr Neuberger attained the age of 100 years in July 2003, and it is reported that he continued to stay engaged in active management of his own accounts, exercised and visited his office daily, throughout his 90s.

> *'You must do something with your life that has meaning for you and for others. Generally, I believe that people who work are happier than those who don't, at any age.'*
>
> ROY R NEUBERGER

> *The story of the Architect's Last Palace tells of an excellent architect who lovingly built many beautiful palaces for the Sultan. Eventually he was tired of his labour and went to the Potentate to ask if he could retire. The Sultan asked the architect to build him one last palace.*
>
> *He said: 'Money is absolutely no obstacle. You have one year to build me the best palace possible.'*
>
> *The architect started eagerly but he was exhausted and the quality of his workmanship began to suffer. He cut a corner here and a corner there. After all, this was his last project and no one would notice. When it came to the materials he used cheaper materials since he could not be bothered to search for the best. After all, who would notice? 'Only himself.' Slowly but surely, the architect started doing less than his best. Eventually, even though no one else could tell the difference, the architect knew that this palace was nowhere near his best. However, he was still pleased that it was complete and at last he could retire.*
>
> *The year had passed and the architect presented his substandard work to the Sultan. The Sultan inspected the palace and was well pleased. When the inspection was over, he turned to the architect and said: 'You have done well. This is my retirement gift to you.'*

> **State Pension Forecast: If you want to know how much State pension you can expect to receive (in today's money values), apply for a State pension forecast. Find out more www.thepensionservice.gov.uk**

Financial life planning questions traditional retirement, believing that you should follow your passions.

> *'Become the change you want to make.'*
>
> MAHATMA GHANDI
1869-1948, INDIAN SPIRITUAL LEADER, WRITER, PHILOSOPHER AND POLITICIAN

Society does little to address the problems of retirement. We need to encourage employers to provide proper retirement planning advice. This might include, for example, the creation of templates that could be used to provide information on important retirement planning issues. We also need to encourage the retention of truly independent financial planners to help us understand the pension scheme on which we are so reliant, investment allocation strategies and generally engage us in retirement transition planning.

In particular, many women retire with lower Social Security and company pension benefits than men, simply because women tend to work for fewer years. Options to make good those lost years must be made available and easily accessible. For too long, knowledge of pension schemes has been left to word-of-mouth opinions and hearsay.

It reminds me of playing Chinese Whispers as a child: the game where you stand in a long line, the first person whispers a phrase to the second who in turn whispers it to the third, and so on. Finally, the last in line shouts out what he thought the phrase was and you all fall about in fits of laughter at how far from the original it is. Of course there's always one guy in the middle who changes things and adds rude words on purpose — but wasn't that half the fun?

A foreign scholar and his entourage were passing through the town. The scholar asked to speak with the most knowledgeable person living there. Of course the townsfolk immediately called for Nazrudin.

The foreign scholar didn't speak Turkish and Nazrudin didn't speak any foreign languages, so the two wise men had to communicate with signs, while the others looked on with fascination.

The foreigner, using a stick, drew a large circle on the sand. Nazrudin took the stick and divided the circle into two. This time the foreigner drew a line perpendicular to the one Nazrudin drew and the circle was now split into four.

He motioned to indicate first the three quarters of the circle, then the remaining quarter. To this, Nazrudin made a swirling motion with the stick on the four quarters.

Then the foreigner made a bowl shape with two hands side by side, palms up, and wiggled his fingers. Nazrudin responded by cupping his hands palms down and wiggling his fingers.

When the meeting was over, the members of the foreign scholar's entourage asked him what they talked about.

'Nazrudin is really a learned man,' he said. 'I told him that the earth was round and he told me that there was an equator in the middle of it. I told him that three quarters of the earth was water and one quarter of it was land. He said that there were undercurrents and winds. I told him that the waters warm up, vaporise and move towards the sky. He said that they cool off and come down as rain.'

Nazrudin's people were also curious about how the encounter went. They gathered around. 'This stranger

> *has good taste,' Nazrudin started to explain. 'He said that he wished there was a large tray of dessert. I said that he could only have half of it. He said that the syrup should be made with three parts sugar and one part honey. I agreed, and said that they all had to mix well. Next, he suggested that we should cook it on a blazing fire. And I added that we should pour crushed nuts on top of it.'*

If our pension planning weren't such a serious matter we, too, could laugh at some of the bold assumptions we make.

Let me tell you a true story that might frighten you a little.

> *Jim MacDonald came to see me in September 1999. This is his story. He and his wife, Susan, had discussed his early retirement, secure in the knowledge that he would receive a 'full pension and tax-free lump sum' based on his loyal service with his employer, ABC Marketing Plc.*
>
> *Like many people, Jim had never read up on his pension scheme, although there was a pension scheme booklet available to all employees and reprinted each year. But he did know that it was a final-salary scheme, and he had often heard it referred to as a Rolls Royce pension, and the best you can get. His employer had stuck with the final-salary scheme, even though Jim knew the company was under pressure by its US parent to move to something called a money purchase group personal pension scheme, which Jim understood to be not as good as what he had. It was apparently all down to something about guarantees.*
>
> *Susan was excited about their early retirement and had secretly been planning how they would spend each of the next five years. Travelling was high on the agenda, safe in the knowledge that the mortgage could be paid off and a handsome pension paid each month. Susan had recently handed in her notice in anticipation of Jim's retirement. These were exciting times and it felt as if all Jim's hard work and long hours had finally paid off.*
>
> *Jim was Marketing Director. The company was very successful and had many long serving employees. Many, like Jim, had worked for 20 years, some even longer, for the 25-year-old Glasgow company. Jim joined the pension scheme on his thirtieth birthday, in September 1979.*
>
> *Jim knew from speaking with others in his situation that these final-salary schemes provided a maximum pension of two thirds of one's final-salary plus a lump sum of one-and-a-half times the final-salary. Jim did not understand why these schemes had to be so complicated but believed he was smart enough to follow the arithmetic.*
>
> - *Salary £ 120,000 x 2/3^{rds} = £ 80,000 per annum, PLUS*
> - *1.5 x £ 120,000 = £ 180,000 as a tax-free lump sum.*
>
> *Jim and his wife had remortgaged regularly to pay for holidays, cars and the cost of sending their two daughters to university in Edinburgh. Fortunately, the mortgage was only £ 175,000 and so they would soon be debt free! A perfect start to retirement.*
>
> *The difficulty with this situation was that Jim had spoken with the company's HR Director the day before our meeting. Jim had been given my name by the HR Director and advised to rethink his retirement plans. I was intrigued.*
>
> *Jim's conversation with David, the HR Director, had gone a bit like this:*
>
> *'Morning, David. I'm here to speak about early retirement — next month in fact. Susan and I have talked it through and have decided we should see a bit more of the world before it's too late. As you know, the girls have almost finished*

university and we feel it's our time now.'

David began explaining how the company's final-salary pension scheme worked and how Jim's pension benefits would be calculated.

'I don't need to know all that,' said Jim. 'I've worked it out already, I'm due £ 80,000 per annum and £ 180,000 as a lump sum, just enough to pay off the mortgage.'

David looked a little worried and asked Jim to slow down. He would explain the details of the scheme.

David explained how Jim's pension was based on his pensionable salary and how this was defined in the company pension scheme booklet. Pensionable salary had been defined, on establishing the scheme, as salary not including bonuses or overtime. Although Jim had earned in excess of £ 100,000 for as long as he could remember, he knew that under this definition his salary was only £ 60,000. The rest was performance-related bonus.

Jim quickly did the sums in his head.

- *Salary £ 60,000 x 2/3^{rds} = £ 40,000 per annum (half of what he had told Susan)*

David also explained that the pension was based on length of service with the company.

'I know that,' said Jim. 'I've been here longer than most and I know that I'm due the maximum two thirds.'

'Well,' said David, 'it doesn't work quite like that.'

Jim's faced dropped. 'What do you mean?'

'Well, yes, you have been here longer than most, I agree. You'll have 20 years' service on your birthday. The scheme is referred to as a sixtieths scheme, which means that you get 1/60 of pensionable salary for each year of service with the company. You've banked 20 years, so 20/60… a third.'

Again, Jim quickly did the sums in his head.

- *Salary £ 60,000 x 1/3rd = £ 20,000 per annum (a quarter of what he had told Susan)*

David went on, 'And if you do decide to retire early, we'll be paying the pension ten years earlier than planned.' With leaden heart, Jim remembered that the normal retirement age for the scheme was age 60. 'So, the early retirement factors will kick in,' David added.

'What do you mean, early retirement factors?' asked Jim.

'Well,' said David, 'we reduce your pension to reflect the fact that the scheme will need to disinvest assets to pay you the pension. In your case this means the scheme effectively losing ten years of anticipated investment growth. These figures are worked out by the pension scheme actuary. It's a fine balance between matching the scheme assets with anticipated liabilities.'

'Oh,' said Jim, gloomily. 'There's a lot more to this than I realised.'

'The early retirement factor in your case is a simple 5% per year reduction in benefits. You would be going 10 years early, so that's a 50% reduction in pension,' said David.

David could see Jim working the figures out in his head.

- *Salary £ 60,000 x 50% reduction = £ 30,000 per annum*
- *Salary £ 30,000 x 1/3 = £ 10,000 per annum (an eighth of what he had told Susan)*

David also explained that Jim's pension would be taxable, as earned income. This meant that effectively the pension was like a salary and that income tax would be deducted at source.

Jim was shocked. His plans to travel the world flashed before his eyes. How would Susan feel about all this?

Jim stood up and looked David squarely in the eyes, clearly shaken. 'Well, at least the mortgage will be paid off.'

'Oh dear,' said David. 'You'd better sit down.'

This was when David gave Jim my name and suggested he get in touch.

What Jim had also failed to appreciate was that the pension scheme paid a pension with the option to 'commute' pension for tax-free cash. What this means is giving up some pension in order to receive a tax-free lump sum. It is not payable in addition to the pension — and this is normal for most private sector final-salary schemes in the UK. It was going to be nowhere near £ 180,000.

Jim didn't wait to hear that final calculation. Close to tears, he left David's office and headed for home.

Sadly, Jim and Susan divorced earlier this year. Ironically, his pension may be further reduced by a pension splitting order issued as part of any divorce settlement. Jim never became a client of mine — he still works for ABC Marketing Plc — but I sense things will never be quite the same again.

If you are in a final-salary pension scheme, don't put your head in the sand like Jim. Look out your pension scheme booklet and arrange an appointment with your HR department. Get the facts while you still have time on your side to do something about it.

You may be interested to know that the UK Government uses a single factor of 20:1 for valuing *defined pension benefits* — those similar to Jim's. Put simply, this means that a pension of, say, £ 50,000 gross per annum will require an investment of around £ 1 million.

Let's assume that someone retiring today and requiring a pension representing two thirds of the average UK wage (which is currently around £ 26,000 per year) payable throughout retirement. They will need to have set aside somewhere in the region of £ 350,000. That's a staggering figure for many people to comprehend, bearing in mind that so many of us expect to retire on far larger pensions than the two thirds average income basis of this calculation.

Financial life planning is a wholly new approach. Many of the same calculations will be carried out, but the advice will be more akin to counselling, helping and planning the transition, hopefully well in advance. There is little reason why some careers should not go on and on, perhaps slowing a little.

As you move ever closer to what can be life's greatest transition, you will need to know your genuine strengths. This will include the reality of how others see you. What skills and qualities do people respect you for?

It's never too late to plan for the future. Identify your potential and begin nurturing your life to create opportunities. Look to understand yourself, to value yourself, and to become the person you really want to be.

Please now re-read *Chapter One: Progressive Life Planning & Management* as a complement to the following questions.

You should record your score in **The WealthFlow System Scoring Table** and **Monthly Progress Chart** in the Appendix.

NOTE: If you honestly feel that a question is not relevant to your current situation, award yourself 10 points. Be honest with yourself! Scoring 'Not Applicable' too often will only mislead you, and draw you into a false sense of financial security.

Answer the following questions by ticking the appropriate box and calculating your score as follows:

10 points = Yes/Agree/Not Applicable
5 points = Not sure/Agree Sometimes
0 points = No/Disagree

QUESTIONS: **Retirement & Life Transition Management**	**Answers** *(please tick)*	**Scoring**
p a s t		
1. Have you kept copies of old pension scheme booklets explaining the benefits you will receive from previous employers' pension schemes?	o Yes *(10)* o Not Sure *(5)* o No *(0)*	
2. Do you or your professional advisers review the annual statements received from previous employers' pension schemes?	o Yes *(10)* o Not Sure *(5)* o No *(0)*	
3. Have you completed death benefit nomination forms in respect of each pension plan/scheme?	o Yes *(10)* o Not Sure *(5)* o No *(0)*	
4. Do you know how well your existing pension funds have performed to date, relative to their peers?	o Yes *(10)* o Not Sure *(5)* o No *(0)*	
5. Have you received independent retirement planning advice in the past?	o Yes *(10)* o Not Sure *(5)* o No *(0)*	
p r e s e n t		
6. Are you happy with the working relationship you have with your pension advisers?	o Yes *(10)* o Not Sure *(5)* o No *(0)*	
7. Are you currently saving for your long-term future?	o Yes *(10)* o Not Sure *(5)* o No *(0)*	
8. Is your current level of savings adequate to provide you with long-term financial security?	o Yes *(10)* o Not Sure *(5)* o No *(0)*	
9. Are you aware of the income tax savings available to those investing into pension plans/schemes?	o Yes *(10)* o Not Sure *(5)* o No *(0)*	
10. Is the investment strategy of your pension assets consistent with your current attitude to risk, and time remaining until you take benefits?	o Yes *(10)* o Not Sure *(5)* o No *(0)*	

11.	Will you be debt free, including mortgage, by the time you fully retire?	o Yes *(10)* o Not Sure *(5)* o No *(0)*	
12.	Do you know where your pension documents are stored and can they be accessed quickly?	o Yes *(10)* o Not Sure *(5)* o No *(0)*	
13.	Do you know the annual rate of return you need from your investments in order to maintain your lifestyle and keep ahead of inflation?	o Yes *(10)* o Not Sure *(5)* o No *(0)*	
14.	Do you know the level and type of death benefits payable from your pension schemes/policies?	o Yes *(10)* o Not Sure *(5)* o No *(0)*	
15.	Are your pension policies in trust?	o Yes *(10)* o Not Sure *(5)* o No *(0)*	
	f u t u r e		
16.	Do you understand how your pension will be taxed, once it starts being paid to you?	o Yes *(10)* o Not Sure *(5)* o No *(0)*	
17.	Have you at least considered the likelihood of working part time in your later years?	o Yes *(10)* o Not Sure *(5)* o No *(0)*	
18.	Have you decided at what age you will start drawing pension benefits?	o Yes *(10)* o Not Sure *(5)* o No *(0)*	
19.	Have you considered what changes you will make to expenditure in later life?	o Yes *(10)* o Not Sure *(5)* o No *(0)*	
20.	Have you considered the attractions of downsizing the family home in later life?	o Yes *(10)* o Not Sure *(5)* o No *(0)*	

21.	Have you thought through whether there are any health issues that will affect your life expectancy?	o Yes *(10)* o Not Sure *(5)* o No *(0)*	
22.	Have you considered the likelihood and impact of receiving an inheritance in later life?	o Yes *(10)* o Not Sure *(5)* o No *(0)*	
23.	If you are in business, have you thought through how your business could become 'sellable' in order to generate capital or an income in later life?	o Yes *(10)* o Not Sure *(5)* o No *(0)*	
24.	Is it clear which of your investments will provide an income in later life?	o Yes *(10)* o Not Sure *(5)* o No *(0)*	
25.	Do you have a clear vision of how you will invest your time and energy when you finally reduce your working hours (retire)?	o Yes *(10)* o Not Sure *(5)* o No *(0)*	
		WealthFlow System Score	**/ 250**
			%

TOTAL PERCENTAGE SCORED AND ITS SIGNIFICANCE	
85 – 100%	Your approach to Retirement Planning should meet your objectives
65 – 84%	Your approach to Retirement Planning needs more effort
Under 65%	Your approach to Retirement Planning needs to be reviewed

CASE STUDY I

Deciding What Is Important

'I've been a gymnast since I was ten years old. My Dad first introduced me to the sport and I haven't been able to stop competing since. So, when I was old enough, I opened a teaching facility and sports shop close to my local club. I have done well financially through the years, and I lead a comfortable lifestyle while keeping the sport — and memories of my Dad — close to my heart.

'However, I am now 50 and often think about retiring — preferably within the next ten years. My motivation is to travel Europe, watching and judging gymnastic competitions.

'In order to do that, I worked with my professional adviser to develop a growth-orientated investment strategy. As well as personal pension policies, I have PEPs and ISAs and a separately managed unit trust portfolio. A second property was purchased two years ago in order to create an income-producing asset for my retirement. After taking advice I recently invested offshore, in the Isle of Man, in order to defer any income until retirement. Excess earned income is invested on a monthly basis to ensure that I save as much as I can.

'I have taken out a permanent health insurance plan to provide much needed peace of mind against the impact of illness and loss of income, and I'm discussing with my adviser the attractions of critical illness cover, too.

'I plan to maximise my annual personal pension contributions. But I am still concerned with two things — reaching my financial goals and maintaining my current lifestyle. I want to be sure that the nest egg I create will allow me to live my retirement dreams — and more.

'That's why I'm glad my adviser informed me of the ability to carry-forward for up to six years the pension relief that has not been utilised in previous tax years. Apparently, because I have an old-style personal pension policy I can do this.

'My adviser has helped me place my retirement goals well within reach, and the best part of all is that I am now free to concentrate on what is most important — teaching my students.'

MISS AB, LONDON

CASE STUDY II

How Much Is Enough?

George came to me for advice a few years ago. He had been approached by a Bolton-based firm offering to buy his business outright. They were keen to have a Scottish base for future developments at Rosyth Dockyard, near Edinburgh. He wasn't sure what his business was truly worth nor indeed what was 'enough' to allow him to retire, live his desired lifestyle and never have to work again.

His accountant had arranged a meeting with the potential buyers the following day. However, George wanted an independent perspective on this and so he called me.

The accountant had told George that it was all about 'hard negotiation' and that he, the accountant, would *not accept a penny less than the business was worth.*

George was not sure that he wanted to enter into hard bargaining over a business he had inherited as a boy and which employed many of his close friends.

George and I sat down and looked at his entire financial position, warts and all. Using financial planning software we were able to project forward George's likely income and expenditure, taking account of all the planned holidays and gifts to family and friends. George had always said he wanted his family (and one or two close friends) to benefit from the sale of the business when he finally retired.

We worked out that George could sell the business for £2.4m and do everything he ever wanted throughout the next 40 years - we made the assumption that he would live to age 100.

The interesting point was that George's accountant had no idea what George 'needed', only that he would 'play hardball' to get the highest sum possible. This was the accountant's only measure of success. He didn't really know George. He didn't know about George's plans to gift money, or his holiday plans for the next 10-15 years. He didn't know that many of George's best friends would continue to work in the business and so it was not all about the money. The accountant simply crunched the numbers and thought he was doing a jolly good job for George.

Financial planning is a dynamic process - it's about much more than number crunching.

The next day, George met with his accountant and the potential buyers of his business. George was adamant that he would only sell if he liked the look of the people and felt comfortable that they would look after his employees.

As the day wore on, a figure of £3.9m was placed on the table. The accountant was unhappy with the offer, stating that based on his figures the business was worth far more. The accountant said that, in his professional judgement, George should hold out for £4.5m or walk away.

However, George liked these people, they were very genuine and had exciting plans for his business. It would mean job security for his workforce.

George was personally delighted with the offer. Why? Because he knew from our financial life planning discussions that he could fulfil his dreams with £2.4m. He urged his accountant to accept the £3.9m along with a list of conditions surrounding pay, pension and perks for his loyal workforce. Reluctantly, the accountant returned to the negotiating table and the deal was struck.

George remains my client and we often laugh at what would have happened if he had rejected the offer. He might still be working. We last laughed about this whilst playing golf in sunny Spain. It really wasn't a bad decision to sell the business after all.

PERSONAL COACHING TIPS

Ensure that you understand, perhaps with the help of your professional advisers, the following key areas:

- The normal sources of income, other than returns on investments, available during retirement
- The major characteristics of State pension provision
- The pension planning opportunities open to you
- The main characteristics of Self Invested Personal Pensions, income withdrawal and phased retirement
- The amount you are eligible to invest tax efficiently
- The limitations of pension products
- The tax treatment of personal pension plans
- The types of 'pension splitting' available to the courts upon divorce

Notes / Doodles

Tax Planning and Mitigation Programme | CHAPTER 06

> *'Death and taxes and childbirth! There's never any convenient time for any of them.'*
>
> MARGARET MITCHELL
> 1900–1949, AMERICAN NOVELIST

Assuming you don't have a background in taxation, the word *tax* probably strikes fear into your heart. Tax planning is simply a way of maximising the amount of money available so that you are free to spend more (or invest more) of your money on the things you enjoy.

Originally, personal tax advice was dispensed by the family solicitor. More recently, this has become the domain of the accountant. However, most individuals do not employ an accountant either to deal with their tax affairs, or to obtain tax advice. This often results in the financial planner taking responsibility for tax planning and mitigation.

Whenever new clients come to my office, they inevitably arrive with years of investment valuations, bank statements, policy and trust documents, with-profits bonus statements and even unopened letters going back months, sometimes years. So much of their financial past was a muddle that it was difficult for them to see clearly their financial present, let alone their financial future. If you were a client I'd want you to use the self-assessment tax deadlines (September and January) as an annual excuse to spring-clean your finances, bringing them totally up to date.

Remember, whomever you select to help with your tax return, you remain the person responsible to the Inland Revenue for getting the return in on time and paying the right amount of tax. April 5 is the last day of each tax year; a new tax year starts on each April 6.

'The Lord giveth and the Inland Revenue taketh away.'

ANONYMOUS

One day, the tax collector of Aksehir and surrounding towns fell into the river. Since he didn't know how to swim, he was about to drown. The villagers gathered by the river bank trying to save him.

'Give me your hand! Give me your hand!' they were all shouting. But the man was not extending his hand. At that time Nazrudin happened to be passing by.

'Mullah Nazrudin,' said the anxious villagers, 'the tax collector fell into the water. He is going to drown. He is not giving his hand!'

'Let me try,' said Nazrudin. 'My friend!' he yelled to the man bobbing in the water. 'Take my hand! Take it!' At this, the tax collector immediately extended his hand and grabbed Nazrudin's arm. Nazrudin and the people around were now able to pull him from the water.

'You see,' Nazrudin clarified, 'he is a tax collector. He is better at taking than giving.'

Taxation is one of the most obvious enemies of your financial future. When you are building an investment portfolio, it is absolutely imperative that you take into consideration your potential tax liability. Investments held within tax-exempt 'wrappers' help your nest egg to grow faster.

The difference on your investments over a 10-to-30 year period can be significant. It can mean the difference between financial pain and financial pleasure. Over a typical 30-year period, if we compare a net return of 6% and a gross return of 7% per annum compound, on £10,000 invested at the outset you could be talking about a monetary difference of £18,688 (£76,123 - £57,435). On £100,000 invested at the outset, this would mean a difference of over £180,000.

'Rich bachelors should be heavily taxed. It is not fair that some men should be happier than others.'

OSCAR WILDE
1854-1900, PLAYWRIGHT

There are three principal taxes in the UK: Income Tax, Capital Gains Tax (CGT) and Inheritance Tax (IHT).

Few people can escape the clutches of Income Tax. Unless you don't work and have few savings, it is unavoidable. The general rule is that if you earn money in any capacity, then you will pay Income Tax on it. It is also levied on many sources of income beyond what is earned at work — for example, savings and dividends on shares.

On average you work three hours of each workday, just to pay taxes. In the United States they refer to *Tax Freedom Day* — meaning that every cent they earn, from January 1st until this day, goes out on taxes. After Tax Freedom Day, they are earning for themselves.

Tax Freedom Day provides an easy way to gauge the overall tax take. In the UK, the March 2004 Budget moved our Tax Freedom Day from 28 May in 2003, to 30 May in 2004. This might look as if it is just two days extra — but with 2004 being a leap year, it's actually three days more. That's three days more of the year that we have to work for the Government, rather than for ourselves.

Tax Freedom Day 2004 fell on 30 May.

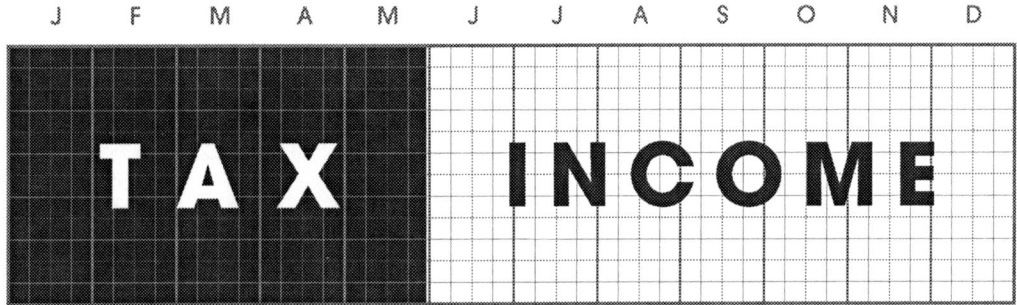

CGT is paid when an individual or company makes a profit by selling or transferring assets to someone else. This could be anything from shares to a painting or a holiday home. Everyone has an allowance before they become liable to CGT. So, if you own anything of value and decide to sell it, you could be presented with a tax bill.

> *'Pay tax on what you take, not what you make.'*
>
> WARREN BUFFETT

About £ 1.4 billion too much IHT is paid each year, according to research from advisers' body, IFA Promotion. The 2003 report revealed that nearly 270,000 estates will be applying for probate, with assets totalling £ 41 billion. It is estimated that £ 2.4 billion will go to the Inland Revenue — but as much as £ 1.4 billion of this could be legally avoided. The good news is that most people do not pay IHT and the Inland Revenue says that in 2001 over 96% of estates avoided it. But it is an area of growing importance for many people.

> *One day, the oppressor Timur was in the mood for teasing Nazrudin.*

'Nazrudin,' he asked, 'can you teach your donkey how to read and have him advise me on how best to reduce my estate taxes?'

'Yes I can, great Timur.'

'Come now, Nazrudin! How can you teach a donkey to read?'

'If you give me three years and 3,000 gold coins, then I can teach my donkey how to read.' Nazrudin was adamant.

'But if, in three-years time, your donkey cannot read, then I will punish you most severely for trying to mock the great Timur.'

Nazrudin and Timur agreed on the terms. Nazrudin took the 3,000 gold coins and left Timur's luxurious tent. Nazrudin's friends who witnessed the deal were incredulous.

'Nazrudin, what have you done? You know you can't teach a donkey anything other than braying. Three years from now, Timur will have your head chopped off!' However, Nazrudin was not worried.

'My dear fellows,' he said calmly, 'before the three years are up, either I will die or Timur will die. Or else, the donkey will die!'

Taxation affects most financial decisions. Financial life planning requires fluency in investments, taxation, risk management, estate planning, pensions and employee benefits, accounting, psychology and motivation. Nevertheless, of all the factors, taxation, in my opinion, is the heart and soul, the nucleus, of financial planning. Tax is the essential ingredient that interrelates all the financial planning disciplines.

Estate Planning & Management Programme		Progressive Life Planning & Management
Tax Planning & Mitigation Programme	**TAXATION**	Breakthrough Cash & Credit Management
Retirement & Life Transition Management		
Savings, Investment & Risk Integration		Personal Risk Management Programme

One piece of advice is to get organised. With self-assessment taxation, you'll need to keep track of every bit of paper generated. In particular, pay special attention to the many documents generated by your investments, dividends and capital gains. Create files, and be meticulous about keeping your records current.

'The avoidance of taxes is the only intellectual pursuit that carries any reward.'

JOHN MAYNARD KEYNES

One of the basic principles of tax avoidance is to ensure that all individuals fully utilise the tax allowances that are available to them. A necessary background to this is an understanding of how the tax system works, including:

AVOIDANCE OF INCOME TAX

Your professional adviser will be best placed to advise you on specific income tax-saving products. These include:

- Individual Savings Accounts (ISAs)
- National Savings
- pensions
- offset mortgages
- buy-to-let mortgages
- single premium investment bonds
- immediate vesting annuities

More sophisticated options include:

- the more exotic property reversion schemes
- Funded Unapproved Retirement Benefit Schemes (FURBS)
- Enterprise Investment Schemes (EISs)
- Venture Capital Trusts (VCTs)

AVOIDANCE OF CAPITAL GAINS TAX (CGT)

The first thing to do is ensure that you fully utilise your annual CGT allowance each tax year. You should also consider specific CGT-saving products. These include:

- zero dividend investment trust shares
- buy-to-let mortgages
- Government gilts
- Permanent Interest-Bearing shares (PIBs)
- Traded Endowment Policies (TEPs)

More sophisticated options include:

- deathbed planning
- share options
- Alternative Investment Market (AIM) shares
- Self-Select ISAs
- EISs
- VCTs

AVOIDANCE OF INHERITANCE TAX (IHT)

Once you have established an up-to-date Will, you may wish to consider making gifts in order to reduce your taxable estate prior to death.

Giving shares to charity is not a new idea, but since April 2000 there is a new tax incentive to make *share giving* even more attractive. Individuals who give shares to charity are entitled to claim back full tax relief against the value of those shares. So, a gift of shares worth £ 1,000 will only cost a higher-rate taxpayer £ 600, or £ 780 for basic-rate taxpayers. What's more, the donor won't be liable for tax on any capital gains.

If you have inherited shares, and know that you should sell them for sound investment reasons, but are caught by the emotional attachment of what these shares represent, *share giving* could be the push you need to dispose of them tax efficiently whilst helping good causes at the same time.

Trusts, as mentioned earlier, should be considered. Assuming your estate is large enough, the simple use of a *nil rate band trust* can save over £ 100,000 of IHT. In addition, life assurance often has a significant part to play. If policies are written under trust, large IHT-free funds can be left on death and such funds can be used to pay any IHT liability that remains. If you are a business owner or hold unquoted shares, including AIM listed shares, *business property relief* should be considered.

OFFSHORE STRATEGIES

Investing offshore can be a very efficient tax option, particularly if you are a higher-rate taxpayer. Offshore investment bonds are available to UK residents in various guises, allowing opportunities for things like the deferral of taxation until maturity, when the penalty will be taxation of the whole gain as income.

INVESTING FOR CHILDREN

You may be surprised to know that the tax system works in much the same way for a four year old as for a 44 year old. From an investment perspective, many of the investments you will consider personally can be accessed for children. Do not think that you must confine your selection to those products specifically targeted at children — although these do have a role to play.

The questions raised at the end of this chapter may lead you to question your past decisions. I hope they will also enable you to ask ever more searching questions of yourself and your professional advisers.

> '*The best effect of any book is that it excites the reader to self-activity.*'
>
> THOMAS CARLYLE
> 1795–1881, SCOTTISH AUTHOR, ESSAYIST AND HISTORIAN

It is a strange feature of the British psyche that we dislike asking the difficult questions. Our reactions to the subjects of taxes and money probably make the psychology of money taboo — just as one's sexuality was a forbidden subject until fairly recently.

People may share their frustrations about not having enough money or about paying too much tax, but never the details of their finances, their behavioural problems with money, or how it makes them feel. If you really want to offend someone, ask how much he or she makes, exactly how much they pay in taxes and how much they spend!

Remember, direct and indirect taxes will often equate to a take of far more than 40% of your earnings. Now you can see why controlling — and ideally mitigating — taxes (legally, of course) is a key component of the WFS.

> *'The difference between tax avoidance and tax evasion is the thickness of a prison wall.'*
>
> DENIS HEALEY
> CHANCELLOR OF THE EXCHEQUER 1974-1979

The chances are that you will want to utilise every legal option available to you to keep your tax burden at a minimum. You must, however, understand that many tax-saving techniques entail a level of investment risk that you may not be willing to accept. You must decide how long you are happy to leave money tied up in investments, and not readily convertible into cash.

A chapter on tax would not be complete without commenting on the use of trusts. Many people are apprehensive over the use of trusts; perhaps rightly so.

Trust is an emotive word which implies integrity and utmost faith; whereby *trustees* are effectively people who control other people's property, having legal responsibility that transcends everything else in life. They are responsible for carrying out the wishes of the Settlor (the person creating the trust) with regard to, and for the benefit of, the beneficiaries.

> *'No, I don't understand my husband's theory of relativity, but I know my husband, and I know he can be trusted.'*
>
> ELSA EINSTEIN (DIED 1936)

The trustees effectively hold the key to the trust 'box'. The trustees will open the box at the appropriate time and deliver its contents to the beneficiary, or beneficiaries, as directed by the Settlor.

When it comes to financial planning the decision of when to use a trust is paramount; although a blanket approach should never be taken. Trusts, when used well, can save tens of thousands, or even hundreds of thousands, of pounds in IHT. They are not, however, solely the province of the very well off, indeed both businesses and families may be candidates for trusts to resolve all manner of problems.

Here are a few examples of how you might use a trust:
- To provide support for your spouse after your death, while protecting him or her from requests by a future spouse for assets, and protecting your assets for your children and grandchildren

- To transfer assets for the benefit of a beneficiary, such as a child or grandchild, while at the same time protecting those assets from a current or future spouse of the beneficiary
- To provide support for, but protect the underlying assets from, a spendthrift or incompetent beneficiary
- To manage your business affairs for you

Those are just some basic uses of trusts. You can tailor a trust to suit your specific needs and objectives, or even various trusts to work together. In light of the complexity of individual circumstances a solicitor should usually be involved.

Controlling the level of tax you pay is one of the most positive steps you can take. Tax planning is typically an area of great frustration. Often a tax return will be filed away and forgotten. You become annoyed by your apparent inability to take action.

If this happens to you, you're not alone. This is a simple example of how we can easily sabotage our own financial life, stopping us from reaching our true potential.

You may need to seek professional help, or it may be that a simple tax planning software package is the answer. Tax planning can debilitate us on two fronts. First, we have to get organised, and gather together the paperwork we need. Second, we have to address our perception that it is all very difficult and dull. The good news is that, like most things financial, it's never as tough as the professionals would have you believe.

The secret is to take control of your tax return and allow yourself the opportunity to transform your financial life.

As you work through this next set of questions, you are again encouraged to reflect on your answers and work out ways to improve your current position.

The following questions should be answered and scored regularly. Please record your score in **The WealthFlow System Scoring Table** and **Monthly Progress Chart** in the Appendix.

NOTE: If you honestly feel that a question is not relevant to your current situation, award yourself 10 points. Be honest with yourself! Scoring 'Not Applicable' too often will only mislead you, and draw you into a false sense of financial security.

Answer the following questions by ticking the appropriate box and calculating your score as follows:

10 points = Yes/Agree/Not Applicable

5 points = Not sure/Agree Sometimes

0 points = No/Disagree

QUESTIONS: **Tax Planning and Mitigation Programme**	**Answers** *(please tick)*	**Scoring**
p a s t		
1. Have you taken the opportunity to invest in Personal Equity Plans (PEPs) and/or Individual Savings Accounts (ISAs)?	o Yes *(10)* o Not Sure *(5)* o No *(0)*	
2. Have you considered the merit of gift aid?	o Yes *(10)* o Not Sure *(5)* o No *(0)*	
3. Have you considered the tax savings associated with *offset mortgages*?	o Yes *(10)* o Not Sure *(5)* o No *(0)*	
4. Are you clear on which of your existing life policies are in trust and which are not?	o Yes *(10)* o Not Sure *(5)* o No *(0)*	
5. Have you invested in pension schemes/policies?	o Yes *(10)* o Not Sure *(5)* o No *(0)*	
6. If so, have you considered establishing a trust to receive lump sum death benefits from pension policies?	o Yes *(10)* o Not Sure *(5)* o No *(0)*	
p r e s e n t		
7. If you are married, are your assets held tax efficiently between husband and wife?	o Yes *(10)* o Not Sure *(5)* o No *(0)*	
8. Do you know on which day the tax year ends?	o Yes *(10)* o Not Sure *(5)* o No *(0)*	
9. Do you know the closing date for submitting a self-assessment tax return to the Inland Revenue, if you want them to calculate your tax liability?	o Yes *(10)* o Not Sure *(5)* o No *(0)*	
10. Do you know the maximum that can be invested into an Individual Savings Account (ISA) in a tax year?	o Yes *(10)* o Not Sure *(5)* o No *(0)*	

11.	Do you fully utilise the tax allowances available to you, for example your annual capital gains tax allowance?	o Yes *(10)* o Not Sure *(5)* o No *(0)*	
12.	Do you know how much you are eligible to invest in pension schemes/policies?	o Yes *(10)* o Not Sure *(5)* o No *(0)*	
13.	Have you discussed with your advisers whether taxes can be reduced through better portfolio management?	o Yes *(10)* o Not Sure *(5)* o No *(0)*	
14.	Do you appreciate that *cash*, as well as stocks and shares, can be held within an Individual Savings Account (ISA)?	o Yes *(10)* o Not Sure *(5)* o No *(0)*	
15.	Are you aware of how much income tax you pay each year?	o Yes *(10)* o Not Sure *(5)* o No *(0)*	
16.	If you are in business, do you ensure that the business pays your pension contributions?	o Yes *(10)* o Not Sure *(5)* o No *(0)*	
17.	Do you know the circumstances in which your children's investment income will be treated as yours for tax purposes?	o Yes *(10)* o Not Sure *(5)* o No *(0)*	
18.	Do you understand how tax relief works in respect of contributions to pension policies/schemes?	o Yes *(10)* o Not Sure *(5)* o No *(0)*	
19.	Do you take tax advice before gifting assets?	o Yes *(10)* o Not Sure *(5)* o No *(0)*	
	future		
20.	Do you know that children can invest in a stakeholder personal pension and receive tax relief?	o Yes *(10)* o Not Sure *(5)* o No *(0)*	

21.	Do you know how your pension tax-free cash lump sums are calculated upon retirement?	o Yes *(10)* o Not Sure *(5)* o No *(0)*	
22.	Do you know the tax bracket that you are most likely to fall into throughout retirement?	o Yes *(10)* o Not Sure *(5)* o No *(0)*	
23.	Are you happy with your current tax advisers?	o Yes *(10)* o Not Sure *(5)* o No *(0)*	
24.	Have you considered the tax benefits of Self Invested Personal Pensions *(SIPPs)* and *income drawdown*?	o Yes *(10)* o Not Sure *(5)* o No *(0)*	
25.	Do you understand the pros and cons of investing offshore for tax deferral purposes?	o Yes *(10)* o Not Sure *(5)* o No *(0)*	
		WealthFlow System Score	/ 250
			%

TOTAL PERCENTAGE SCORED AND ITS SIGNIFICANCE	
85 – 100%	Your approach to Tax Planning should meet your objectives
65 – 84%	Your approach to Tax Planning needs more effort
Under 65%	Your approach to Tax Planning needs to be reviewed

Donations To Charity

'Last January, I decided to give some cash to a local charity that supports children with learning difficulties. My logic was that a cash donation would be the simplest and best approach for everyone.

'I happened to mention this to my professional adviser and she showed me how I could use the assets within my investment portfolio — avoiding capital gains tax.

'What I did was donate some highly-performing unit trusts to the charity. The entire amount was treated as a charitable donation. Had I used available cash, and then sold that unit trust to cover another expense, I would have paid capital gains tax on the sale.

'Working with my professional adviser, I developed a number of fundamentally sound, tax-reducing strategies — including taking advantage of opportunities presented by my investment portfolio — that have helped me reduce my tax liabilities and maintain my cash reserves in case of emergencies.'

Mr PPJ, Aberdeen

PERSONAL COACHING TIPS

Ensure that you understand, perhaps with the help of your professional advisers, the following key areas:

- The broad principles relating to income tax and capital gains tax planning
- The most tax efficient ways of supporting charitable work financially
- The circumstances when a liability to capital gains tax arises
- The taxes which arise during transfer of capital during life
- The impact of domicile and residence on capital taxes
- The options available to you in order to maximise tax efficiency

Notes / Doodles

Estate Planning and Management Programme | CHAPTER 07

> *'It is hereby certified that the gross value of the said estate amounts to £ 21,468,352.'*
>
> THE WILL OF DIANA, PRINCESS OF WALES, MARCH 1998

Princes William and Harry faced an £ 8.4 million inheritance tax bill on the estate of their late mother, Diana, Princess of Wales. The problem arose because their mother had not drawn up a new Will that took into account the £ 17 million settlement that she had received following her divorce. Surprisingly, none of the monies had been placed in trust for her sons.

A word of caution: Even experienced professional advisers make mistakes when it comes to implementation. One of the most common errors is to give insufficient time to *estate planning*.

If you haven't yet sorted out your affairs, now is the time to act!

Estate planning could be described as *'the passing of as many assets as possible to those most important to you'*; or, less attractively, as *'the separation of you and your money, as soon as possible, forever'*. The good news, however, is that it doesn't have to be that way.

> **NOTE: Your net worth (your assets minus your liabilities), plus death benefits and certain trust property, constitute your estate.**

In this chapter it is assumed that you want to control your property whilst alive and well, to care for yourself and your loved ones, and to be able to give what you want, to whom you want, the way you want, when you want. Also, it is assumed that you want to save all the tax, solicitor's fees and legal costs possible.

The only certain way to maintain control after you've met the Grim Reaper is to draw up a Will. Unfortunately, many people ignore this truth. In fact, according to some estimates, as many as two thirds of those in the UK die *intestate*, which means without a valid Will.

Think of a Will as a five-year rolling project and make amendments to it as your life changes. The obvious times to revisit the terms of your Will are:

- on marriage or divorce
- if you have a child
- when you buy a home
- if you establish a business
- retirement
- if one of your heirs dies
- when any of your children becomes financially independent

Also, simple things like completing death benefit nomination forms is often overlooked. It is, of course, human nature to avoid thinking about such unpleasant things — but who is going to answer these questions when you're gone?

Why bother to name your beneficiaries?

Well, when you name the beneficiaries for your life insurance policies or retirement plans, the money goes directly to those individuals after your death. If you name no beneficiaries, the money probably goes to your estate, to be distributed according to your Will. This can be costly (solicitor/legal fees) and time-consuming. Moreover, depending on estate size, your heirs may have to pay estate taxes, which could devour up to 40% of the estate's assets. Thus, inappropriate planning can be very costly.

> **Whole of life policies, written in trust, which provide a capital sum on death, are often employed to fund the likely inheritance tax liability, regardless of when death occurs. For married couples this typically means a 'joint life last survivor' policy, as it is on the survivor's death that the majority of inheritance tax will fall due.**
>
> **Knowing that there will be enough cash available, on death, to pay inheritance tax should provide peace of mind. Your beneficiaries need not be forced to sell family assets at the *wrong time* (shares in a falling market, or property in a housing slump) to pay inheritance tax.**

Completing a death benefit nomination form assumes that the policy has been placed in some form of trust. Although one of the most attractive features of life insurance is that the death benefits are free from income tax and capital gains tax, this does not mean you also automatically escape estate taxes (inheritance tax).

Unless life insurance is written under trust, the policy's death benefit will be considered to be part of your estate and taxed accordingly. Be careful when placing long-running life insurance policies in trust for the first time. This could have immediate tax consequences.

You may be wondering whether your Will is going to take care of all this. Your Will takes a back seat to beneficiary designations. Thus, if you name someone as the beneficiary of a life insurance policy, that person gets the money no matter what your Will says. In other words, don't assume your Will can 'fix' any old beneficiary designations you've either forgotten about or no longer want in place. Problems can easily arise, for example with a previous partner whom you no longer wish to benefit. The simple answer is to ensure that beneficiary designations are kept up-to-date.

What about gifting? Many people find that money is a powerful tool for doing good. As the mania for accumulation appears to have slowed, people are becoming more focused on their real values — particularly since the events of September 11, 2001, the avalanche of corporate accounting scandals, and in the wake of the economic downturn.

Older investors appear more willing to work with philanthropy in their estate plans, as money is now widely perceived by the affluent as something that can solve problems. This is an area where personal values rise quickly to the surface, such as fears over outliving one's wealth, passing too much money to unappreciative children or siblings, and personal views on taxation and mortality.

> *'He who does not give what he has, will not get what he wants.'*
>
> HENRY III
> 1207-1272, KING OF ENGLAND

For many *baby boomers* (those born between 1946 and 1964, the next generation of retirees), good estate planning carried out by thoughtful parents will lead to a burst of sudden wealth. However, sudden wealth comes at a high price for those psychologically unprepared for the pressure of having it all.

Some people feel estranged from their friends because of their newfound-wealth, or may be wondering how they should deal with relationships now that circumstances have changed. Other people spend, spend, spend, with no rhyme or reason to their spending. At the end of the day, there are a lot of issues to address.

> *'To be at once exceedingly wealthy and good is impossible.'*
>
> PLATO
> C.429-C.347 BC, GREEK PHILOSOPHER

Being clear about your own financial goals, and defining your family's core money values, are what's needed here. Among the first things to do is to prepare or update your Will.

Tough decisions need to be made. Authors Susan Bradley and Mary Martin (*Sudden Money: Managing a Financial Windfall*, John Wiley & Sons) refer to a *Decision-Free Zone*, a period of six to 12 months or more, during which no major decisions are made about the money. Instead, the emphasis should be placed on planning, dealing with fears and getting rid of confusion.

Sudden wealth is not always welcomed. John, a £ 1.3 million UK Lottery winner gave away his wealth two days before Christmas. He feared the impact it would have on his close family.

'Outside it was snowing, and I saw a group of Salvation Army collectors with buckets, singing Christmas carols. The snow was falling on me and I began to cry. The snow felt really clean. I crossed the street, took out the private banking chequebook that I had been assigned and wrote out the cheque, placing it in the bucket.' John's cheque was cashed the following week.

'It all felt so easy and right. I have no regrets,' he says with a smile. John had hoped to win around £ 500, to pay off a loan from a close friend.

Philanthropy may be the answer. Educate yourself about non-profit organisations and how they might benefit from your benevolence. Also, assess whether you would be best served by creating your own foundation. You can control your wealth, get attention in the community, and do good. It's a *gain-gain* situation.

> '*One of the serious obstacles to the improvement of our race is indiscriminate charity.*'
>
> ANDREW CARNEGIE
> 1835-1919, SCOTTISH-BORN PHILANTHROPIST

> *Nazrudin took employment as a prayer leader in a town other than his own. In this town there was a tradition. People saved gold coins and when they had enough to fill up an earthenware jar, they buried the jars in their gardens. Once a year, they dug up the vessel, looked at their coins and then buried them again. When Nazrudin learned about this practice, he found an earthenware jug, filled it with pebbles and buried it.*
>
> *'Dear sir, that won't do,' said the townsfolk. 'You are supposed to fill it with gold.'*
>
> *'Good people,' Nazrudin laughed, 'considering that you don't spend the money you own, what difference does it make if it is gold or pebbles?'*

You could create a hypothetical shopping list of things that your heirs might buy with the money you are leaving them. Doing this might reveal that you're leaving so much money that the children will never have to work another day in their lives. Of course, this is not necessarily a bad thing — but realising this may lead you to recognise the potential impact of your legacy.

Lastly, a touch of reality. Far more people are anticipating inheritances than will actually receive them. The reasons are obvious:

- Most people don't have wealthy parents

- Much of the wealth of our parents is in the form of pensions, whereby on death the money dies with them

- People are living longer than ever and they're increasingly spending all their money during their extended lifetimes. A rule of thumb, that appears to hold true, is to expect that 95% of the lifetime cost of medical care is incurred in the last four or five years of a typical individual's lifetime — and 50% in the final year

  Let's take an example. A 65 year old can expect to live to 81, while an 85 year old can expect to live to 90. Such long life expectancies virtually guarantee a person's involvement in their parents' personal finances: paying bills, managing savings and perhaps helping to secure and pay for long-term care services. We are quickly approaching a society where, instead of money being passed from father to son, it's going from daughter to mother. Yet despite these intense relationships, there is a remarkable lack of communication about finances between the generations.

- Many older people see their children and grandchildren doing nicely, much better than they did at their age, and so are reluctant to spoil them

- As we're all living longer, there are more heirs around looking for a slice of grandmother's money. Let's assume that grandmother decides against gifting money whilst alive, and decides that her children should wait until her death to receive an inheritance, just as she did. The difference is that grandmother probably received her inheritance in her thirties, assuming her parents died in their fifties. Today, a grandmother living to age 90 will leave her children when they are in their sixties, and her grandchildren in their thirties — and they will perhaps have children of their own.

'How sharper than a serpent's tooth it is to have a thankless child!'

KING LEAR, ACT I, SCENE IV, BY WILLIAM SHAKESPEARE

It is worth noting that, as we have seen already, even if you do receive an inheritance you may have to wait months, or even years, until such time as the estate is wound up and assets distributed. It all depends on the level of estate planning carried out. When you do finally benefit, if the inheritance is held in trust then you may only be entitled to receive an income and no capital, or vice versa. Don't assume you know how and when the inheritance will be paid.

The reason for raising these issues is simply to deliver words of caution. Most people would be best advised to ignore the possibility of reaching their goals as a direct result of gifts or inheritances.

Congratulations on reaching this final section! You are, I hope, well on your way to making significant improvements to your financial life. I'm sure you have surprised yourself with your refreshed state of mind. I hope terms such as *spending plan or budget, savings, pensions, tax* and *life insurance* have become less frightening or frustrating. You really are capable of taking charge of your financial life.

In this final section we have looked at estate planning. This is one area that I would encourage you to discuss with a solicitor, and make a point of keeping all your other advisers aware of what you are up to. So much of good tax planning is about tying up all the loose ends. Fully-informed advisers are more likely to save you tax, and on death to save your estate time and money in carrying out your final wishes.

Be aware that professional advisers make a lot of money in fees from poorly-organised estates. Think about it: if this weren't such a profitable area for professionals, particularly solicitors, you would be asked to pay an awful lot more for having a Will drafted at the outset. Think of it as professional marketing, a sprat to catch a mackerel.

Controlling the level of professional fees and estate taxes should be important to you, since a poorly-organised estate ultimately means less of your money is left to be passed on to loved ones.

A chilling point to ponder is that, by the time your poorly-organised estate comes to light, after your death, it's too late for you to complain.

As you work through this final set of questions, please continue to reflect on your answers and think through ways to improve your current and future positions.

The following questions should be answered and scored regularly. Please record your score in **The WealthFlow System Scoring Table** and **Monthly Progress Chart** in the Appendix.

NOTE: If you honestly feel that a question is not relevant to your current situation, award yourself 10 points. Be honest with yourself! Scoring 'Not Applicable' too often will only mislead you, and draw you into a false sense of financial security.

Answer the following questions by ticking the appropriate box and calculating your score as follows:

10 points = Yes/Agree/Not Applicable
5 points = Not sure/Agree Sometimes
0 points = No/Disagree

Questions: **Estate Planning & Management Programme**	**Answers** *(please tick)*	**Scoring**
p a s t		
1. Have you considered any inheritance tax saving strategies in the past?	o Yes *(10)* o Not Sure *(5)* o No *(0)*	
2. Have you considered establishing a *Power of Attorney*?	o Yes *(10)* o Not Sure *(5)* o No *(0)*	
3. Have you prepared a detailed inventory of assets and liabilities to determine your estate's value?	o Yes *(10)* o Not Sure *(5)* o No *(0)*	
4. Do all your assets have the correct beneficiary clearly defined?	o Yes *(10)* o Not Sure *(5)* o No *(0)*	
5. If you are in business, have you considered the impact of your business assets on your estate planning?	o Yes *(10)* o Not Sure *(5)* o No *(0)*	
6. Have you considered the use of trusts in your estate planning?	o Yes *(10)* o Not Sure *(5)* o No *(0)*	
p r e s e n t		
7. Do you know your likely financial loss to inheritance tax in monetary terms?	o Yes *(10)* o Not Sure *(5)* o No *(0)*	
8. Are you satisfied with your current level of charitable giving?	o Yes *(10)* o Not Sure *(5)* o No *(0)*	
9. Is your Will current, and is it less than five years old?	o Yes *(10)* o Not Sure *(5)* o No *(0)*	
10. Do you understand the consequences of dying intestate?	o Yes *(10)* o Not Sure *(5)* o No *(0)*	

11.	Do you know the current level of the nil-rate band?	○ Yes *(10)* ○ Not Sure *(5)* ○ No *(0)*	
12.	Do you know the level of inheritance tax in percentage terms that is chargeable on the value of your estate over the nil-rate band threshold?	○ Yes *(10)* ○ Not Sure *(5)* ○ No *(0)*	
13.	Do you appreciate that one-off wedding gifts are a tax efficient way of passing on wealth to children?	○ Yes *(10)* ○ Not Sure *(5)* ○ No *(0)*	
14.	Are the trustees of any trust arrangements still appropriate persons/bodies?	○ Yes *(10)* ○ Not Sure *(5)* ○ No *(0)*	
15.	Is your Will coordinated with your life insurance, investment and pension beneficiary designations?	○ Yes *(10)* ○ Not Sure *(5)* ○ No *(0)*	
16.	Are premiums in respect of life insurance policies paid by the policy trustees?	○ Yes *(10)* ○ Not Sure *(5)* ○ No *(0)*	
17.	Does your estate have sufficient liquidity to meet its immediate cash-flow obligations on your death?	○ Yes *(10)* ○ Not Sure *(5)* ○ No *(0)*	
18.	Have you provided non-binding Letters of Wishes to trustees, regarding the distribution of capital under life assurance and pension policies?	○ Yes *(10)* ○ Not Sure *(5)* ○ No *(0)*	
19.	In the event of your death, would there remain at least two surviving trustees?	○ Yes *(10)* ○ Not Sure *(5)* ○ No *(0)*	
20.	Are you satisfied with the working relationship you have with your solicitor/legal advisers?	○ Yes *(10)* ○ Not Sure *(5)* ○ No *(0)*	

21.	Do you know how much you can gift on a regular basis before it is treated as a *Potentially Exempt Transfer* (PET)?	o Yes *(10)* o Not Sure *(5)* o No *(0)*	
22.	Have you discussed with your parents their wealth transfer plans?	o Yes *(10)* o Not Sure *(5)* o No *(0)*	
23.	Are you aware that very substantial gifts can be made from income, without impacting on future inheritance tax liabilities?	o Yes *(10)* o Not Sure *(5)* o No *(0)*	
24.	Have you considered whether it is prudent for you to gift assets to others during your lifetime?	o Yes *(10)* o Not Sure *(5)* o No *(0)*	
25.	Are you clear about which charities, if any, you favour regarding the investment of your time and energy?	o Yes *(10)* o Not Sure *(5)* o No *(0)*	
26.	Have you considered the financial consequences of requiring long-term care?	o Yes *(10)* o Not Sure *(5)* o No *(0)*	
27.	Do you feel you have sufficient practical knowledge on which to make meaningful decisions?	o Yes *(10)* o Not Sure *(5)* o No *(0)*	
28.	Are you clear about who will get what, once you're gone?	o Yes *(10)* o Not Sure *(5)* o No *(0)*	
29.	Have you considered the future financial security of your dependants?	o Yes *(10)* o Not Sure *(5)* o No *(0)*	
30.	Are you aware that by making use of each spouse's inheritance tax nil-rate band, you can potentially create a tax saving on death of over £ 100,000?	o Yes *(10)* o Not Sure *(5)* o No *(0)*	

	WealthFlow System Score	/ 300
		%

TOTAL PERCENTAGE SCORED AND ITS SIGNIFICANCE	
85 – 100%	Your approach to Estate Planning should meet your objectives
65 – 84%	Your approach to Estate Planning needs more effort
Under 65%	Your approach to Estate Planning needs to be reviewed

Case Study i

Death Bed Planning

In the previous chapter I made reference to deathbed planning. Let me explain.

Some years ago, it became clear that a close friend had only a short time to live. His wife had been very successful in business and had built up substantial wealth.

Her investment portfolio was pregnant with significant capital gains, which with quick thinking gave way to a significant tax-saving opportunity for the family. The assets were transferred to her dying husband, with the arrangement for them to be bequeathed back to her by Will★.

Her husband received the investment portfolio at original base cost, in the knowledge that the investments would be uplifted to market value on his death. Therefore, when they were eventually transferred back to her, a new base cost had been established and no capital gains tax was due.

There was no inheritance tax liability, since transfers between spouses were, and still remain, exempt.

A tax saving of around £ 70,000 was made, providing his young family with additional financial security.

★ You should always seek legal advice concerning Wills.

Case Study ii

Family Responsibilities

'Saturday, August 27, 2003. I'll never forget that date. It was the day I literally saw my life flash before my eyes.

'It was almost noon and we were making our way back from the hockey match. It had rained all morning, but lightning was nowhere in sight. So, needless to say, it caught us by surprise when a bolt of lightning hit a tree five feet from my car. It really scared me. And although I initially feared for my life, as that shock wore off I began to think, and worry about my husband and children. What if I never got to see them again? What would they do without me? Was I financially prepared for the worst?

'It was after that day that I decided to contact my professional adviser for help in planning my estate. Although she had wanted to include it as part of my overall financial plan, I'd felt that I was too young to worry about dying. I've certainly changed my mind since then.

'My adviser suggested I consider developing three fundamental elements to any estate plan: a Will, a Power of Attorney and a Living Will.

'She said a Will would specify how my assets are to be distributed, who is to serve as executor, and how taxes would be paid from my estate — all important information that would help ease my family's worries.

'Next, she recommended that I develop a Power of Attorney. If I were to become physically or mentally incapacitated, the Power of Attorney would name someone to act on my behalf by making the important legal and financial decisions.

'Finally, she urged me to create a Living Will. This would serve to outline my preferences for medical treatment. If any life-prolonging medical equipment or procedures could be used in case of serious injury or illness, this document clarifies my wishes.

'Although it was a painful topic to broach, I feel confident that my estate plan will help ease my family's emotional trauma and financial burden if I should suddenly die. And although I've since learned not to play hockey in the rain, I'm now sure that you can never be too safe.'

Mrs FRM, Edinburgh

Personal Coaching Tips

Ensure that you understand, perhaps with the help of your professional advisers, the following key areas:

- The potential consequences of dying intestate
- The importance of seeking professional help in drawing up a Will
- The major considerations which need to be taken into account before drawing up a Will
- The reasons why you may wish to set up a trust
- The major characteristics of inheritance tax
- The best use of trusts and life assurance in planning for inheritance tax
- The considerations surrounding a Power of Attorney

Notes / Doodles

Appendix

You can use the WFS to clarify what you truly want from your money. Rather than simply monitoring investment performance as the major factor in achieving your financial objectives, you can decide which objectives you actually want to achieve, thus giving your money real value and creating personal motivation.

Financial life planning is about you, your needs and aspirations. The WFS provides a method of measuring your progress.

WealthFlow Scoring Thresholds Table

	Actual WealthFlow Score	Should Meet Objectives	Needs More Effort	Immediate Review Needed
Breakthrough Cash & Credit Management		85 - 100	65 - 84	Under 65
Personal Risk Management Programme		85 - 100	65 - 84	Under 65
Savings, Investment & Risk Integration		85 - 100	65 - 84	Under 65
Retirement & Life Transition Management		85 - 100	65 - 84	Under 65
Tax Planning & Mitigation Programme		85 - 100	65 - 84	Under 65
Estate Planning & Management Programme		85 - 100	65 - 84	Under 65

WealthFlow Monthly Progress Chart

	Breakthrough Cash & Credit Management	Personal Risk Management Programme	Savings, Investment & Risk Integration	Retirement & Life Transition Management	Tax Planning & Mitigation Programme	Estate Planning & Management Programme
January	%	%	%	%	%	%
February	%	%	%	%	%	%
March	%	%	%	%	%	%
April	%	%	%	%	%	%
May	%	%	%	%	%	%
June	%	%	%	%	%	%
July	%	%	%	%	%	%
August	%	%	%	%	%	%
September	%	%	%	%	%	%
October	%	%	%	%	%	%
November	%	%	%	%	%	%
December	%	%	%	%	%	%

GOAL-SETTING FORM

This form is designed to assist in the process of
defining and achieving your individual goals.
I've included a few examples, to start you off.

Private Goals	State Goal	Track Actions	Start / Finish Dates
Goal 1	*Save On Monthly Basis*	*£ 250 into 'Cash' ISA.*	*Jan 05 - Jan 08*
Goal 2	*Learn German*	*Attend Tuesday Class*	*Dec 04 - Dec 05*
Goal 3	*Give Up Smoking*	*One Cigarette less per week*	*Oct 04 - Jan 05*
Goal 4			
Goal 5			
Goal 6			
Goal 7			
Goal 8			
Goal 9			
Goal 10			

Component Parts	Ongoing Position	Deadline Date	Tick On Completion
05 - £3,000 06 - £3,000 07 - £3,000	*Review performance six-monthly*	*Jan 08 £9,000 plus interest*	
Every Tuesday 5.30 - 9.00pm	*One weekend break to Berlin per month*	*Dec 05 Pass Exam*	
20 weeks	*Review progress monthly*	*31/01/2005 Non-Smoker!*	

SAMPLE CLIENT MEETING AGENDAS

The following sample agendas illustrate how The WealthFlow Partnership conduct client meetings.

In the first instance we will conduct two meetings:

  a. Introductory Meeting

  b. Financial Plan Meeting

INTRODUCTORY MEETING AGENDA

Item 1 – What advice is being sought?

Item 2 – Outline of *The WealthFlow Partnership* Service

Item 3 – Planning Assumptions

Item 4 – Cash Flow Projection

Item 5 – Initial Data Gathering

Item 6 – The Way Forward

Item 7 – Any Other Business

First meeting to be held at The WealthFlow Partnership on Tuesday 2nd March 2005

To be attended by: Chris Consolidation (CC)

                               Duncan R Glassey (DRG)

You will incur no cost or obligation to 'The WealthFlow Partnership' at this meeting.

The aim of this meeting is to provide you with a clear understanding of the practical features and benefits of The WealthFlow Partnership Service and to explain anything that is not made clear in our terms of business/client agreement. This should enable you to decide whether or not you would like to become a WealthFlow client.

The WealthFlow Service

This service offers the ability to model numerous life planning scenarios. What this means is that we are able to demonstrate the impact of a wide range of future events. We will actively involve you in this modelling process and from it an agreed plan of action in the form of the Financial Plan is created. We believe that by involving you in the creation of the Financial Plan in this way, you are placed in a position to make better decisions about the future.

Equity Linked Investment

We believe that by using exclusively pooled investment funds (unit trusts and investment trusts), this will reduce the level of risk to which you are ultimately exposed.

Fee-Basis

We believe that you deserve truly independent financial advice that is not influenced by commissions.

Bridging The Gap

We exist to deliver a highly innovative combination of financial life planning and investment management to you and your immediate family. The service is driven by the latest technology and our commitment to look after your long-term needs.

We believe that for many people the void that exists between their stockbroker or investment manager on the one hand and their various financial advisers on the other is undesirable. We exist to bridge this gap.

For the avoidance of doubt, it should be understood that The WealthFlow Partnership is an independent firm.

Agenda Item	Decisions and Notes
Item 1 - What advice is being sought?	*(see Appendix: Life Transitions Profile)*
Item 2 - Outline of *The WealthFlow Partnership* Service DRG to explain briefly the features and benefits of The WealthFlow Partnership Service. The WealthFlow Partnership Service has five general objectives, in addition to helping you become financially well organised: a. Using *The WealthFlow System*™ – determine specific life goals – the accomplishment of which will lead to a *better life*. b. To help you understand clearly where you are *now* in financial terms. c. To help you to define and cost your desired *future* lifestyle. d. To help you develop and implement a Financial Plan to achieve that desired future lifestyle. e. To help you make sensible provision for possible financial catastrophes.	*The WealthFlow Partnership Service includes ongoing review of your Financial Plan as necessary to take account of changed circumstances.* *Achieving these objectives often involves a combination of investment planning, tax planning, risk management and estate planning – embodied within The WealthFlow System*™.

Agenda Item	Decisions and Notes
Item 3 - Planning Assumptions DRG to explain the importance of using realistic and sensible assumptions. It will be necessary to agree with you a whole range of planning assumptions before a comprehensive Financial Plan can be finalised. However, we use a very structured approach to agreeing these planning assumptions and the process is usually painless and, indeed, interesting.	*We work on the basis that if the planning assumptions cannot be faulted the conclusions that flow from them should normally be accepted.*

Item 4 - Cash Flow Projection
 	
DRG to explain the importance of producing lifelong Cash Flow Projections.
	WealthFlow Cash Flow Projections almost always provide 'early warnings' of one of two situations. Either:
	
	    a. On the stated assumptions, you will need to use investment capital to balance your budget – you may eventually run out of money, or
	
	    b. On the stated assumptions, you will see a steady increase in the value of your investment portfolio.
	
	In either case financial planning issues arise. If there is a danger of running out of money it will be necessary to increase cash inflows and/or reduce cash outflows. If, on the other hand, the value of investments seems likely to keep increasing, Inheritance Tax may become an issue, which in turn will throw up opportunities for estate planning.
	
	Action taken in response to the 'early warnings' can deal with potential problems before they become severe enough to destroy your chance of a secure financial future.

Agenda Item	Decisions and Notes
Item 5 - Initial Data Gathering DRG to produce for you a preliminary analysis of your current position. This analysis should enable you to judge whether The WealthFlow Partnership Service will be beneficial and will represent good value for money.	
Item 6 - The Way Forward If you decide that you would like to become a WealthFlow client – to complete the necessary documentation and agree a date for next meeting.	

Agenda Item	Decisions and Notes
Item 7 – Any Other Business How did you hear about The WealthFlow Partnership? Actions: 1. The WealthFlow Partnership request commitment from you through the signing of an agreement and payment of an establishment fee. 2. You are asked to provide details of your assets, liabilities, income and expenditure within 10 days of this Introductory Meeting. 3. Once in receipt of these details we analyse your current financial position in advance of the Financial Plan Meeting. 4. Date set for Financial Plan Meeting, typically within three weeks of the Introductory Meeting.	

FINANCIAL PLAN MEETING AGENDA

Item 1 – Compliance with the Rules of the FSA and Money Laundering Regulations

Item 2 – Working with other Professional Advisers

Item 3 – General Points in need of Clarification

Item 4 – Overview of Principal Issues

Item 5 – Personal Objectives

Item 6 – Planning Assumptions

Item 7 – Current Cash Flow Management

Item 8 – Future Cash Flow Management

Item 9 – Key Financial Assets

Item 10 – Current Asset Allocation / Investment Returns

Item 11 – Investment Policy Statement

Item 12 – Asset Allocation to meet Desired Returns

Item 13 – Tax Efficient Asset Wrappers

Item 14 – Estate Planning

Item 15 – Catastrophe Risks

Item 16 – Service Standards

Item 17 – Action List

Item 18 – Arrangements for Next Meeting

Second meeting to be held at The WealthFlow Partnership on Fri. 2nd April 2005 at 9am

To be attended by: Chris Consolidation (CC) – age 46 on 01/12/2005
                                Kate Consolidation (KC) – age 46 on 17/07/2005
                                Duncan R Glassey (DRG)

The WealthFlow Service

This service offers the ability to model numerous life planning scenarios. What this means is that we are able to demonstrate the impact of a wide range of future events. We will actively involve you in this modelling process and from it an agreed plan of action in the form of the Financial Plan is created. We believe that by involving you in the creation of the Financial Plan in this way, you are placed in a position to make better decisions about the future.

Equity Linked Investment

We believe that by using exclusively pooled investment funds (unit trusts and investment trusts), this will reduce the level of risk to which you are ultimately exposed.

Fee-Basis

We believe that you deserve truly independent financial advice that is not influenced by commissions.

Bridging The Gap

We exist to deliver a highly innovative combination of financial life planning and investment management to you and your immediate family. The service is driven by the latest technology and our commitment to look after your long-term needs.

We believe that for many people the void that exists between their stockbroker or investment manager on the one hand and their various financial advisers on the other is undesirable. We exist to bridge this gap.

Agenda Item	Decisions and Notes
Item 1 - Compliance with the Rules of the FSA and Money Laundering Regulations • Check that the latest version of our terms of business/client agreement has been signed. • To ensure that we have photocopies of relevant documents to satisfy Money Laundering Regulations.	
Item 2 - Working with other Professional Advisers • Whilst The WealthFlow Partnership Service is broad in scope, we appreciate that you may have other professional advisers in respect of tax and legal matters. We ask for their details in case you require us to communicate with them in the future.	
Item 3 - General Points in need of Clarification • Communication by email Check that we have the correct email address for confidential communication. • Agency transfers Decide whether existing policies or investment products should be transferred to our agency. This will allow us to take on the servicing responsibility. • WealthFlow Fees Our fees will always be agreed with you in advance.	

Agenda Item	Decisions and Notes
Item 4 - Overview of Principal Issues DRG to outline what appear to be the principal issues to be addressed at this meeting.	• *Help establish desired lifestyle goals.* • *Review of all assets and personal cash flow.* • *Identification of risks to your financial security.* • *Reduction of personal and estate taxes.* • *Achievement and/or maintenance of your desired lifestyle.* • *Organisation of your financial affairs.*
Item 5 - Personal Objectives Your Major Definite Purpose? We need to clearly understand your principal objective over the following 12 months. Please indicate which of the following objectives are most important to you. • Financial Independence • Basic Family Security • Income Tax Planning • Investment Planning • Your Children's Education • Investing for Children • Estate Planning • Business Protection • Gifts to Charities • Planning for Retirement • Other	*Please rank the selected objectives in order of personal importance.*

Agenda Item	Decisions and Notes
Item 6 – Planning Assumptions	
• Future inflation: 2.6% pa?	
• Future growth in the value of tax advantaged assets: 6% pa?	
• Future growth in the value of other equity linked assets: 5% pa?	
• Future growth in the value of property: 5% pa?	
• Age at which pension benefits will be taken? (current assumption CC's 65th birthday)	*(WealthFlow Financial Modelling - affordability of early retirement)*
• KC's 'death in retirement' pension to be what percentage of CC's pension? Assumed 50%?	*(WealthFlow Financial Modelling - financial impact in retirement)*
• Total return, after tax, on cash awaiting long-term investment: 1.3% pa?	
• Plans for future house moves?	*(WealthFlow Financial Modelling - benefits of downsizing)* *See Diagram*
• Date of sale - second/other properties?	*(WealthFlow Financial Modelling - determining when to sell)*
• Planning assumptions regarding cars?	
• Future gifts from parents?	*(WealthFlow Financial Modelling - impact of family inheritance)*
• State pension benefits?	
• Education expenses?	*(WealthFlow Financial Modelling - the cost of education funding)*
• Investments for children/grandchildren?	
• Planning for retirement?	*(WealthFlow Financial Modelling - achieving & maintaining your desired lifestyle)*

Before Downsizing Main Residence At Age 75 (3/4 value)

Chart: Value of Readily Realisable Assets

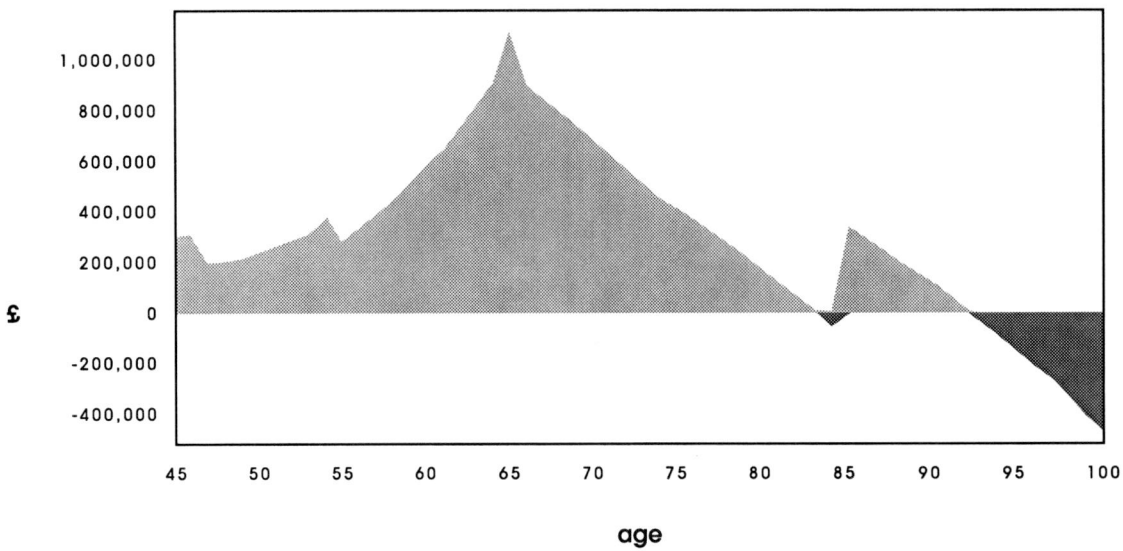

After Downsizing Main Residence At Age 75 (3/4 value)

Chart: Value of Readily Realisable Assets

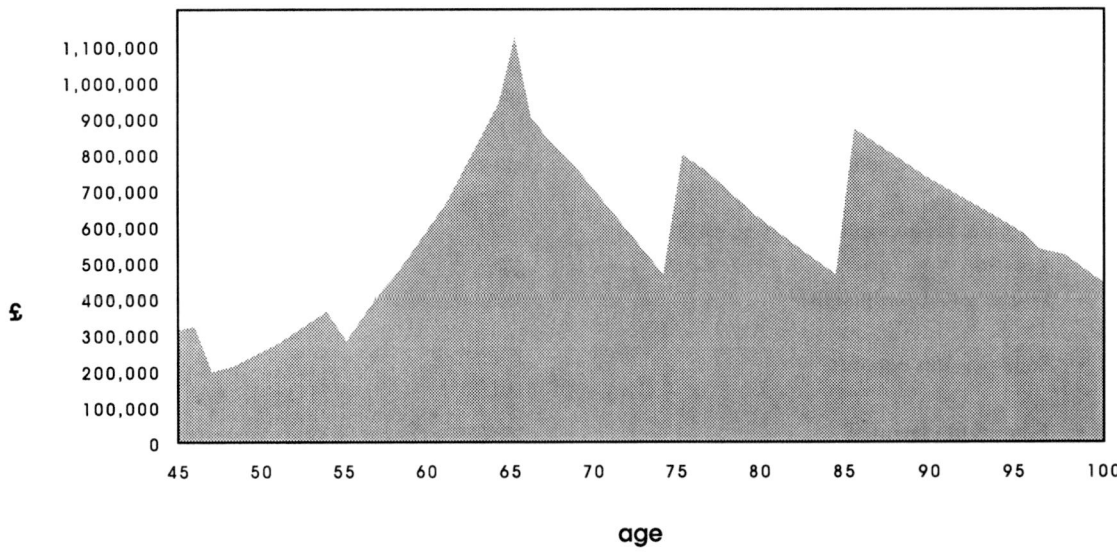

Agenda Item	Decisions and Notes
Item 7 - Current Cash Flow Management Review the summary of current income and expenditure and decide how much surplus income, if any, is available for investment.	*According to the latest information known to The WealthFlow Partnership, it appears that cash inflows currently exceed cash outflows by approximately £ 1,982 per annum.* *(WealthFlow Financial Modelling - current position)*
Item 8 - Future Cash Flow Management Are there any major purchases or special events for which financial planning may be necessary and which have not already been included in the Cash Flow Projection? If so, estimate future cash flow on prudent planning assumptions and decide on any action to be taken. Producing a lifelong Cash Flow Projection is one of the most important features and benefits of The WealthFlow Partnership Service. It identifies whether or not a desired future lifestyle will be financially possible and whether there is a danger of running out of money.	
Item 9 - Key Financial Assets • History of Net Worth • Log of financial assets for review • Assets due to mature within 12 months? • Business Planning Decide on personal income and business profit objectives for the next 12 months. Identify the price at which it may be worthwhile selling the business. • Main Residence Having regard to current interest rates and investment conditions, decide whether to pay off all or part of the existing mortgage.	*(WealthFlow Financial Modelling - price required to achieve and maintain desired lifestyle)*

Agenda Item	Decisions and Notes
	Example: All the assets that we would expect to be transferred to our custody have been back-tested for the past 10 years to determine their risk and return characteristics.
Item 10 - Current Asset Allocation / Investment Returns Review of investment performance and risks associated with ALL existing financial assets.	*The majority of the assets were held in managed-type products with the balance in a portfolio of direct equities managed by a stockbroker.* *When the returns were compared with The WealthFlow Asset Allocation Matrix it was clear that a broadly similar result could have been achieved by simply investing in cash over this period, which would have produced an annual real return of 2.1%. In other words, you have not been rewarded for taking the extra investment risk.* *Had your investment managers reduced their commitment to equities to 70% and merely achieved an index return over the 10-year period, the matrix suggests that they would have experienced a similar level of volatility but a much better return overall.*
Item 11 - Investment Policy Statement It is important that we develop a clear understanding of your attitude to investment risk and that the investment performance expectations are consistent with this attitude. A suitable asset allocation policy can then be agreed – including all personally held assets.	

Agenda Item	Decisions and Notes
Item 12 – Asset Allocation to meet Desired Returns To agree an appropriate asset allocation, having first reviewed the relative merits of: • Cash alternatives • National Savings investments • Fixed Interest/Government Gilt linked funds • Property linked funds • Equity linked funds • Individual holdings • Financial derivatives Note: We do not think that the returns achieved in the equity markets over the past 10 years will necessarily be mirrored in the next 10 years.	*The WealthFlow Matrix highlights that you have been experiencing volatility levels that are consistent with having 70% of your portfolio in equities, whilst the returns have mirrored those of cash deposits.* *You have indicated that you are comfortable with the inherent volatility levels of the current portfolio. We would therefore restructure the portfolio to reflect the 70/30 asset allocation illustrated above. We would then expect to be evaluated on a bespoke benchmark consisting of 70% equity returns and 30% cash equivalent returns.*

EXPECTED RETURN <u>BEFORE</u> RESTRUCTURE OF ASSETS ASSUMING A CONTINUED REAL
RETURN OF 1.9% PER ANNUM

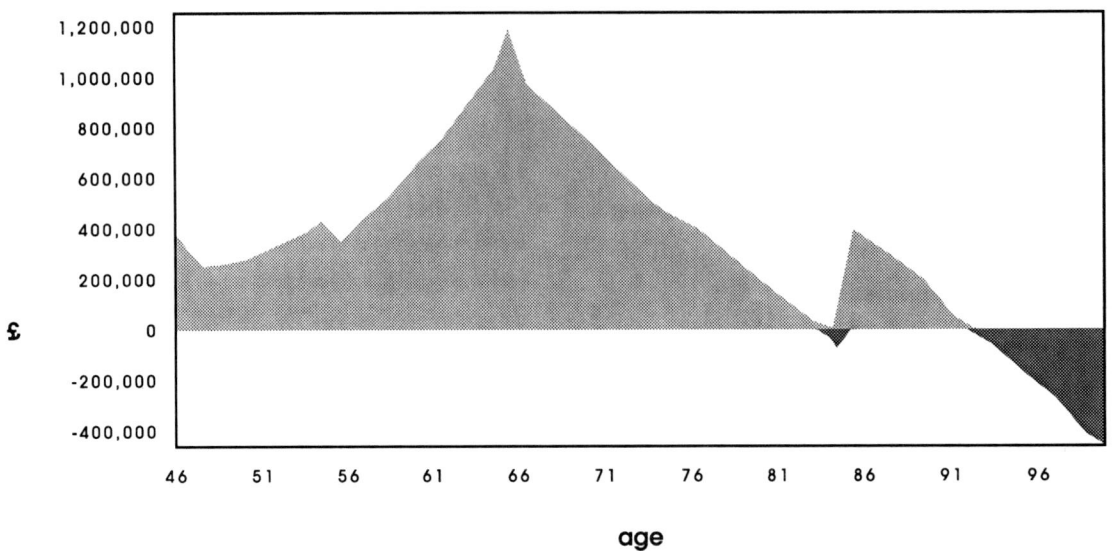

EXPECTED RETURN <u>AFTER</u> RESTRUCTURE ASSUMING
A REAL RETURN OF 6% PER ANNUM IN LINE WITH 70% EQUITY EXPOSURE

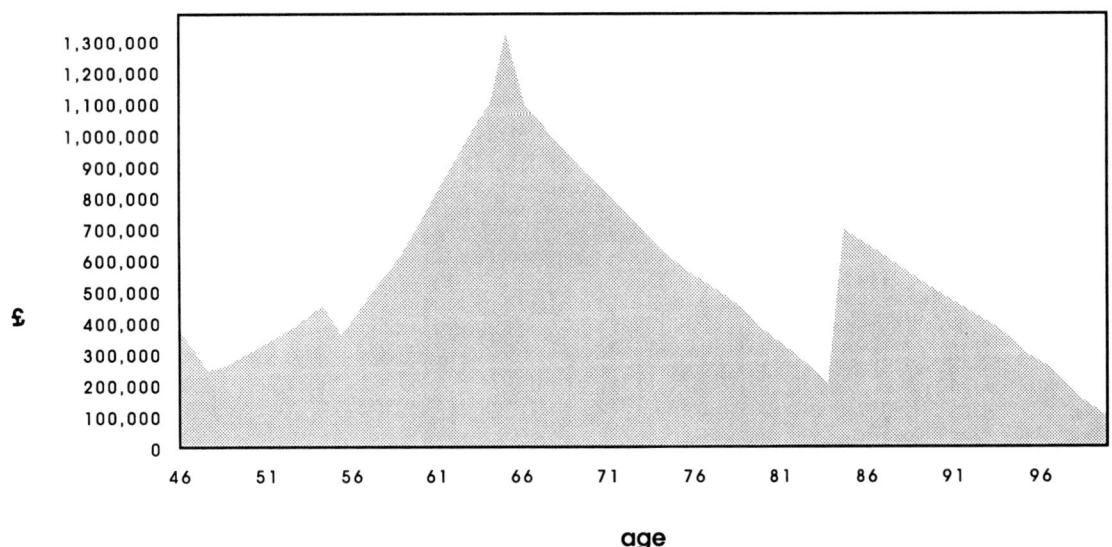

Agenda Item	Decisions and Notes
Item 13 - Tax Efficient Asset Wrappers • Self Invested Personal Pension (SIPP) The WealthFlow SIPP gives you the opportunity to have your pension funds managed alongside your overall investment portfolio. Gains made within the fund are free of CGT. • Individual Savings Account (ISA) An ISA is one of the more valuable and tax efficient entitlements available to you. Currently you can invest up to £ 7,000 a year. Gains are free from CGT and there may be income tax advantages. • Personal Equity Plans (PEPs) You have the option to transfer your existing PEPs to The WealthFlow Partnership. We do not charge for this service. • Life Assurance Bonds Tax deferred annual withdrawals of up to 5% of the sum originally invested can be taken from investment bonds. Money can be switched between the underlying investment funds free from liability to personal tax. • Ten Year Qualifying Investment Plans Investment plans designed to provide tax-free cash or income after 10 years. • Unit Trusts & Investment Trusts Unit and investment trusts offer a simple means of investing in a spread of stock market securities with the benefit of professional fund management. They offer the potential to generate tax-free profits using the annual CGT exemption.	

Agenda Item	Decisions and Notes
• Venture Capital Trusts (VCTs) Income tax relief at 40% is available. The annual investment limit on which tax relief is available is currently £ 200,000, for shares issued on or after 6 April 2004. • Enterprise Investment Schemes (EISs) The annual investment limit for income tax relief under the EIS is £ 200,000 for shares issued on or after 6 April 2004.	*(WealthFlow Financial Modelling - impact of tax favoured return)*
Item 14 - Estate Planning • Decide how much (if any) to gift on a regular basis so as not to be treated as a Potentially Exempt Transfer (PET). • Decide how much (if any) to transfer into an inheritance-tax-free insured Trust Fund for the benefit of family members and/or charities. • Review Wills, review opportunities to reduce potential IHT liability and consider whether there will be sufficient cash available to meet any liability which remains. According to our records, current Wills were last updated in 1999. • Provision for dependants How important is the future financial security of your dependants? • Policy trustees Check that, in the event of the death of both CC and KC there would be at least two surviving trustees.	*Current Position* *Had both died yesterday Inheritance Tax of £ 323,183 would have been payable.* *(WealthFlow Financial Modelling - regular gifts out of income)* *(WealthFlow Financial Modelling - anticipate charge to Inheritance Tax)*

Agenda Item	Decisions and Notes
• Guidance to trustees Check that non-binding Letters of Wishes have been written to guide trustees regarding the distribution of capital under life assurance and pension policies. • Payment of premiums under existing life policies issued under trust Ideally, premiums should be paid by the policy trustees, albeit with money made available to them by the Settlor(s). A separate bank account is desirable. • Powers of Attorney Check that Powers of Attorney have been established.	
Item 15 – Catastrophe Risks • Review of existing policies Review the premiums being charged for existing life insurance policies and establish whether, subject to medical underwriting, better terms would now be available. • Premature death Decide whether there is sufficient life insurance in force. • Disability Review existing arrangements and decide if any action is necessary to ensure that current living standards could be maintained in the event of disability through accident or illness. • Long-term care Decide whether to arrange additional insurance cover to provide for the potential cost of long-term care.	*Current Position* *Based on current planning assumptions: Had Chris or Kate died yesterday, or been disabled and in need of long-term care, there would have been a significant financial problem – See Diagram* *(WealthFlow Financial Modelling - financial consequences of death) – See Diagram* *(WealthFlow Financial Modelling - financial consequences of disability)* *(WealthFlow Financial Modelling - financial cost of long-term care)* *Health checks* *We strongly recommend clients have a comprehensive annual medical examination.*

Position On Death <u>Before</u> Adding Life Assurance Cover

Chart: Value of Readily Realisable Assets

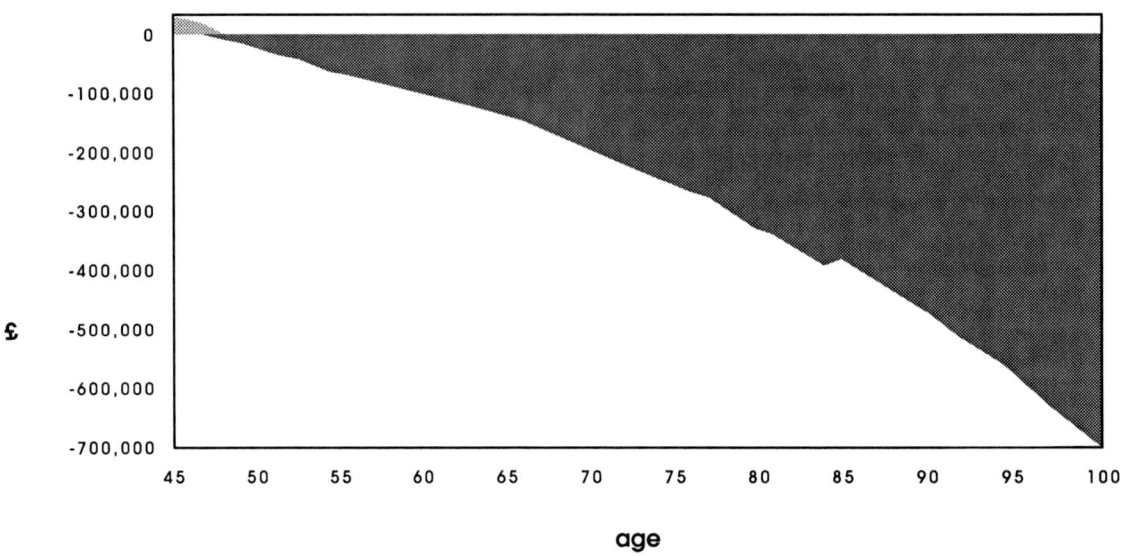

Position On Death <u>After</u> Adding Life Assurance Cover

Chart: Value of Readily Realisable Assets

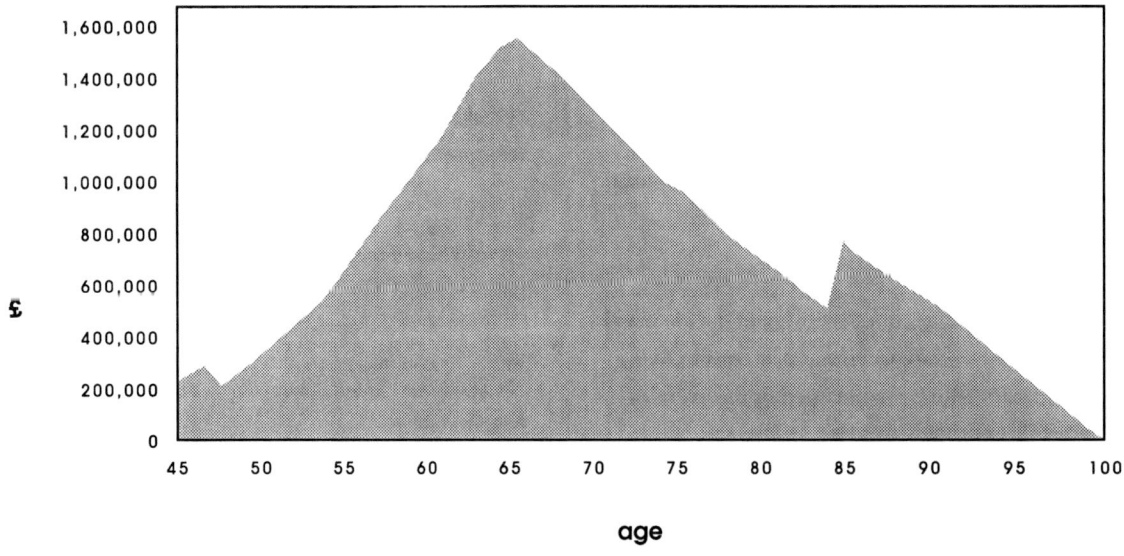

Agenda Item	Decisions and Notes
Item 16 – Service Standards • In what ways do you think we could improve our service in order to provide additional value? • In what ways has it been particularly helpful so far? • Helping others Can we identify friends, family members or colleagues who may like to receive a copy of *'Financial Freedom: Using The WealthFlow System'* and/or an invitation to one of our seminars?	
Item 17 – Action List	

Action	Responsible Person	*Notes/Deadlines*

Agenda Item	Decisions and Notes
Item 18 - Arrangements for Next Meeting • We will write to you 90 days before the annual Financial Plan Review Meeting, requesting up-to-date income and expenditure information. • We will also need information about any changes to your assets or liabilities. • We will prepare an up-to-date valuation of your investments for this meeting. • We will send you the updated Cash Flow statements (and the assumptions behind it) 30 days before our meeting.	*Date: 2nd July 2006 / Time: 9:00am* *Special items to be included on the agenda:*

Life Transitions Profile

Name _____

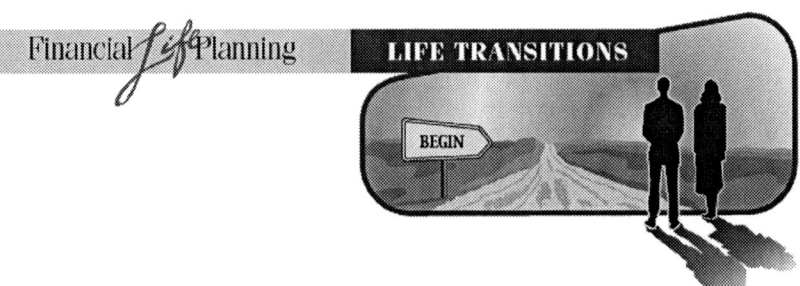

Select the priority level of the life transitions that you are experiencing now or expect to experience in the near future. **Leave all others blank.**

Personal / Family   Priority Level

Getting married	O H	O M	O L
Going through a divorce or separation	O H	O M	O L
Recent loss of your spouse (widowhood)	O H	O M	O L
Expecting a child	O H	O M	O L
Adopting a child	O H	O M	O L
Need to hire child care	O H	O M	O L
Child entering adolescence	O H	O M	O L
Child with special needs (disability / other)	O H	O M	O L
Child preparing for university	O H	O M	O L
Child going away to university	O H	O M	O L
Child getting married	O H	O M	O L
Empty nest	O H	O M	O L
Special family event	O H	O M	O L
Providing assistance to a family member	O H	O M	O L
Concerned about an aging parent	O H	O M	O L
Concerned about the health of spouse or child	O H	O M	O L
Concerned about personal health	O H	O M	O L
Family member in need of professional care	O H	O M	O L
Family member with a disability or serious illness	O H	O M	O L
Family member expected to die soon	O H	O M	O L
Recent death of family member	O H	O M	O L
Recent birth of a child	O H	O M	O L
Family member diagnosed with cancer	O H	O M	O L
Entering single parenthood	O H	O M	O L

Work / Career

Priority Level

Contemplating Career Change	O H	O M	O L
New Job	O H	O M	O L
Job promotion	O H	O M	O L
Job loss	O H	O M	O L
Job restructuring	O H	O M	O L
New job training / education programme	O H	O M	O L
Starting a new business	O H	O M	O L
Gaining or losing a business partner	O H	O M	O L
Selling or closing a business	O H	O M	O L
Transferring business to family member	O H	O M	O L
Downshift / Simplify work life	O H	O M	O L
Taking a sabbatical or leave of absence	O H	O M	O L
Phasing into retirement	O H	O M	O L
Full retirement from current job / career	O H	O M	O L
Buying an existing business	O H	O M	O L
Expanding an existing business	O H	O M	O L

Financial / Investment

Selling a house	O H	O M	O L
Refinancing your mortgage	O H	O M	O L
Purchase a home	O H	O M	O L
Relocating	O H	O M	O L
Reconsidering investment philosophy and risk profile	O H	O M	O L
Significant investment gain	O H	O M	O L
Significant investment loss	O H	O M	O L
Concerned about debt	O H	O M	O L
Considering an investment opportunity	O H	O M	O L
Receiving an inheritance or financial windfall	O H	O M	O L
Selling assets	O H	O M	O L
Considering changing financial service provider	O H	O M	O L

Community / Charitable

Priority Level

Give to other charitable organisations	O H	O M	O L
Monthly stipend to parent(s) (parental pension)	O H	O M	O L
Gifting to children / grandchildren	O H	O M	O L
Develop or review an estate plan	O H	O M	O L
Develop an end of life plan	O H	O M	O L
Creating or funding a foundation	O H	O M	O L
Creating or funding a scholarship fund	O H	O M	O L
Give to community causes / events	O H	O M	O L
Give to church or religious organisations	O H	O M	O L

Notes / Doodles

One Last Thing

Congratulations on making it to the end of this book. That tells me you've taken a lot of this material seriously and are starting to experience deep personal growth.

You may be feeling excited now about discovering what you want from this life. Some of the questions I've asked may have left you squirming; not knowing the answer is never a nice feeling. Our experiences and attitudes about money, often passed down from parents, have a powerful effect on our lives. Some of these are good, others less beneficial.

The chapters of this book represent a real, working system, and provide tools that will help you along the way to financial freedom.

You can now understand some of your past decisions, and uncover *why* you are where you are with money. If you also feel encouraged to think more deeply about your future, then this book has succeeded. Anything that gets us out of our conventional ways of thinking and motivates us to move forward must be worthwhile.

Money is a false god. That seems easy to say now — but I had to travel a journey before appreciating this fully. I hope this book will shorten your own journey, and lengthen your time in a fuller life worth living.

We're all here to learn and pass on our experiences in an attempt to help others. It is my firm belief that we can have almost anything we want, as long as we help enough other people get what they want, too. In Sufi tradition there is a saying: *'I was a hidden treasure, and longed to be known, so I created a world that I might be known.'*

I believe that our use of money reflects our lives like a mirror. I hope this book has raised you to a heightened sense of self awareness, that ultimately inspires and motivates you.

However, if you feel a little unsure of where to go from here, then be grateful for the opportunity to take back control of your financial future. I hope you will eventually feel the benefit of a new-found freedom towards money.

In January 1998, I was passed an email from a colleague at work — one of the many jokes and stories that are always being forwarded around the globe. You may even have received it yourself. I've kept it ever since and every so often I stumble across it, read it again and file it in the hope that I will stumble across it again one day. It reads:

If I had my life to live over again, I'd try to make more mistakes next time. I wouldn't be so perfect. I would relax more. I'd limber up. I'd be sillier than I've been on this trip. In fact, I know very few things that I would take so seriously. I'd be crazier. I'd be less hygienic.

I'd take more chances, I'd take more trips, I'd climb more mountains, I'd swim more rivers, I'd go more places I've never been to. I'd eat more ice cream and fewer beans.

I'd have more actual troubles and fewer imaginary ones!

You see, I was one of those people who lived sensibly and sanely, hour after hour and day after day. Oh, I've had my moments, and if I had to do it all over again, I'd have more of those moments — moment by moment.

I've been one of those people who never went anywhere without a thermometer, a hot water bottle, a mouthwash, a raincoat and a parachute. If I had to do it all over again, I'd travel lighter next time.

If I had to do it all again, I'd ride more merry-go-rounds, I'd watch more sunrises, and I'd play with more children; if I had my life to live over again.

But you see, I don't.

This book is intended to be a wake-up call. Life isn't all about money, and as you decide upon your own direction, this will become clearer. Some of the richest people I know have very little money or outward signs of financial wealth. Often it is these very people whom we aspire to be like. We rarely ask: *why?*

No one is standing in our way. Good luck with your journey. And have lots of fun.

Glossary

Active Management

An investing strategy that seeks returns in excess of a specified benchmark. Investors who believe in active management do not follow the 'efficient market hypothesis'. They believe it is possible to profit from the stock market through any number of strategies to identify mispriced securities. This is the opposite of passive management.

Actuary (actuarial)

A professional person employed, usually, by insurance companies, because they have special skills in calculating insurance rates by reference to the mathematical laws of probability to measure potential risks. In England, these people are members of the Institute of Actuaries; in Scotland they belong to the Faculty of Actuaries.

Alternative Investment Market (AIM)

A market for small, young and growing companies operated by the London Stock Exchange. There are about 400 companies listed on AIM. AIM companies tend to trade on wider spreads than companies on the main market, and liquidity can be a problem. There are tax advantages of investing in AIM companies.

Asset Allocation

The process of dividing a portfolio among major asset categories, such as bonds, stocks, or cash. The purpose of asset allocation is to reduce risk by diversifying the portfolio. The ideal asset allocation differs based on the risk tolerance of the investor. For example, a young executive might have an asset allocation of 80% equity (shares) and 20% fixed income (government and corporate bonds), while a retiree would be more likely to have 80% in fixed income and 20% equities.

Blue Chip

A company on the London Stock Exchange with a large market capitalisation and reputation as a reliable investment. The term is believed to come from the gambling chip used in casinos.

Capital Gains Tax (CGT)

A tax on gains made when you sell assets — things like shares, a holiday home or an oil painting. If you buy an asset or investment then later sell it for more than you paid for it, you are said to have made a capital gain. Make enough gains in one particular tax year and you will be liable for CGT. Everyone is allowed to make a certain level of profit each year before capital gains tax is charged. This amount is known as the capital gains tax allowance and is reviewed annually in the Budget.

Cash

The value of assets that can be converted into cash immediately. This typically means bank accounts and building society accounts.

Cash Flow

The total amount of money being transferred into and out of a personal bank account or building society account, especially as affecting liquidity.

Certified Financial Planner (CFP)

Licence awarded to individuals who successfully complete the CFP Board's initial and ongoing certification requirements. Those wanting to become a CFP professional must take extensive exams in the areas of financial planning, taxes, insurance, estate planning, retirement, among others, and complete continuing education programmes each year to maintain their certification status.

Charitable Trust

A trust which has been registered with the appropriate authority and which enjoys income tax advantages.

Churning

Stockbrokers earn a living from commission. Churning is their way of earning more. It is the highly dubious practice of making a large number of trades within discretionary funds, on the client's behalf. The object of this trading is not to make any money for the client, but to generate commission for the broker. Churning is an offence under the rules governing stockbrokers.

Collective Investment

A collective investment is a fund which takes money from a number of private investors and pools it together. A professional fund manager will then use his or her skill to make investments that should increase the value of the funds under management. Unit trusts, investment trusts and Open Ended Investments Companies (OEICS) are examples of collective or pooled investments.

Corporate Bonds

A corporate bond is an IOU issued by a public company, such as British Telecom, ICI or Marks & Spencer. When you invest in a corporate bond, you are lending money to the company. In return you will receive interest at a fixed rate and the promise that your capital will be repaid at a certain date in the future. The guarantee that your capital will be returned is only as good as the company you are lending money to. While BT, ICI or Marks & Spencer are considered 'good risks' by investment pundits because they are 'blue chip' companies, other, smaller companies are **not** likely to be such a 'good risk'. Most private investors first became interested in corporate bonds when they were made eligible for inclusion in PEPs. You may now invest in corporate bonds via an ISA.

Critical Illness Cover (CIC)

This is insurance which pays out on diagnosis of a critical illness such as cancer, heart attack, stroke or multiple sclerosis. It should be noted that medical treatment for such critical illnesses is usually covered by Private Medical Insurance (PMI) plans. A critical illness benefit is an additional financial benefit, often a lump sum, paid on diagnosis of such critical illness. Critical Illness Cover bridges the gap left by life insurance which only pays out if you die. These days, people are surviving illnesses that were once fatal, but having survived, many people are unable to return to work or find that they have to pay for special medical care.

Day Trading (Day Trader)

An equity (shareholder) 'investor' who holds positions for a very short time (from minutes to hours) and makes numerous trades each day. Most trades are entered into and closed out within the same day.

Dervish

A Sufi religious man who has taken vows of poverty and austerity. Dervishes first appeared in the 12th century; they were noted for their wild or ecstatic rituals and were known as dancing, whirling, or howling dervishes according to the practice of their order.

Discretionary Investment Management

To put it simply, if you choose a service of this kind you will give your manager the authority to buy and sell investments for you without obtaining your prior approval on each and every occasion. One of the major advantages of a discretionary service is that your fund manager will be able to take immediate action in response to changing market conditions — investment opportunities can be missed in the time that it takes to contact clients and ascertain their wishes. For many private client stockbrokers, discretionary management is their flagship service, but some will only offer it to larger clients.

Diversification

When investing there are a few basic rules; one key rule is to not have all your eggs in one basket. In other words, don't invest all your funds in one asset. For example, if you are putting money into shares, buy a selection of companies so that if one performs badly or goes bust, you won't lose all or nearly all of your money. Spread it around — diversify — because this is the best way to spread your risk, and reduce the volatility which might come from holding just one or a very small number of shares. So, if you have just a few hundred or a few thousand pounds, you might feel limited to being only able to realistically buy two or three shares. A good alternative might be to buy a unit trust which tracks the biggest companies in the London stockmarket.

Efficient Market Hypothesis (EMH)

An investment theory that states that it is impossible to 'beat the market' because prices already incorporate and reflect all relevant information. This is a highly controversial and often disputed theory. Supporters of this model believe it is pointless to search for undervalued stocks or try to predict trends in the market. Academics point to a large body of evidence in support of EMH.

Enterprise Investment Scheme (EIS)

The purpose of the Enterprise Investment Scheme (EIS) is to help certain types of small higher-risk unquoted trading companies to raise capital. It does so by providing a range of tax reliefs for investors in qualifying shares in these companies. It does not provide the level of diversification associated with a Venture Capital Trust.

Equity

The risk-bearing part of a company's capital, usually referred to as ordinary shares. The owners of the equity, the shareholders, are the owners of the company and have the right to elect directors and share in the company's profits through the payment of dividends. 'Equity' has a slightly different meaning when it comes to home ownership.

Equity (housing)

In housing terminology, equity is the difference in the value of the property and the amount outstanding on any loan secured against it. If the size of the outstanding loan is greater than the market value of the property, you have negative equity — a situation which became commonplace in the early 1990s. The term 'equity' is used in the stockmarket with a slightly different meaning — see above.

Ethical Investing

Ethical investment seeks to invest in companies which make a positive contribution to the world, and seeks to avoid companies which harm the world, its people or its wildlife. It is difficult for an individual investor to judge whether a particular company is ethical or not. Therefore, most ethical investments are held through a managed investment fund such as a unit trust or life insurance or pension fund. Most UK ethical funds are based on a combination of positive and negative investment criteria. Some emphasise the former, while others concentrate on the latter, and some try to strike a balance between the two.

Fee-based Services

Most financial advisers earn their living by taking a commission from the life insurance or investment companies whose products they sell. This commission must be disclosed to the client and it can be argued that the system has worked reasonably well. That being said, many investors fear that advice from an adviser will be coloured by his or her need to earn commission. It is clear that this has happened in the past with the result that vulnerable investors have been badly disadvantaged. So, some independent financial advisers offer their services as fee-based in much the same way as do accountants and solicitors. They charge the client by the hour or agree a one-off fee upfront. Any commission earned is then rebated or offset against fees due. This can make a lot of sense in view of the fact that there are financial products which would suit you which don't pay your adviser to recommend them.

Fee-only Financial Planning

Fee-only financial planning means that advisers are compensated solely by their clients, and do not accept commissions or compensation of any kind based on the products that they recommend. There's no better way to be confident that your adviser is working solely in your interest. This is a perfect model for financial coaching.

Final-Salary Scheme

In a final-salary pension scheme, the pension you receive will be based on a fraction of your pensionable earnings (those taken into account by the scheme) at retirement. The size of the fraction is calculated by reference to the length of your service in the scheme. Commonly used fractions are one-sixtieth or one-eightieth for each year of service. For example, anybody in a final-salary pension scheme, based on sixtieths, with 40 years of service, would be entitled to a pension of forty-sixtieths or two-thirds of their final-salary (this is the maximum permissible). Retiring early generally means a reduced pension (unless ill health is the cause). Private sector schemes may give you the option of exchanging part of your pension for a tax-free lump sum. The main public sector schemes give you the lump sum in addition to the calculated pension – this being a significant benefit.

Financial Services Authority (FSA)

On 1 December 2001, the FSA assumed its full powers and responsibilities under the Financial Services and Markets Act 2000. It is the single statutory financial regulator in the UK, having taken over the work of a total of nine previous watchdog bodies. Almost all kinds of financial services firms must get permission (authorisation) from the FSA to do business in the UK. The FSA regulates banks, building societies, credit unions, insurance and investment firms (stockbrokers and fund managers) and Independent Financial Advisers (IFAs). The FSA has specific responsibilities to consumers, aiming to help people become better informed about financial matters so that they can manage their financial affairs more effectively.

Fixed Interest

The term generally refers to bonds on which the holder receives a predetermined and unchanging rate of interest. What this offers the potential investor is a known return from holding the investment. That return contrasts with the non-guaranteed variable return from equities.

Footsie

A slang term for the FTSE 100 index. The Footsie consists of 100 'blue chip' stocks that trade on the London Stock Exchange.

FTSE 100

The most widely-quoted and popular index for tracking the London stockmarket. The FTSE 100 contains the shares of the top 100 UK companies ranked by market capitalisation. The FTSE is a market capitalisation-weighted index, re-weighted every day. During the day, it is calculated every minute.

Funded Unapproved Retirement Benefits Schemes (FURBS)

Unapproved pension schemes, or Funded Unapproved Retirement Benefit Schemes (FURBS), are occupational pension schemes that build up retirement benefits in excess of those allowed under approved pension schemes. Employers typically set them up to provide more flexible remuneration packages for high earners. Such schemes do not receive the generous tax reliefs available to approved pension schemes.

Gilts

Sometimes referred to as British Government bonds, gilts are a way for the Government to raise money from large financial institutions like pension funds and from private investors like you and me. The money is needed by the Government because the Treasury so often finds that its outgoings (to pay for things such as road building and unemployment benefit) exceed its income (from things such as taxation). To make matters more confusing, gilts are sometimes referred to as *gilt-edged securities* or *bonds* or *fixed-interest securities*. In any event, gilts are issued by the Treasury and, in nearly all cases, the investor hands over his cash and then receives a fixed rate of interest for the life of the gilt. When the gilt matures, its capital value is repaid at par value.

Higher Rate of Tax

The UK tax system taxes different pounds of our income at different rates. Some income is free of tax (the personal allowance), a chunk of our income is taxed at the lower rate, another chunk at the basic rate, and then the top chunk at the higher rate. This higher rate is set at 40%. As economists say, the UK tax system is a progressive one — meaning that the more you earn, the more tax you pay. You may object to the higher rate of tax at 40% but spare a thought for the previous generation: in the 1974/75 tax year, it stood at 83% payable on income of more than £ 20,000.

Income Tax

Income tax is payable on any income, whether it's derived from working or investment. Every person, however, can earn a certain amount of money each year before tax kicks in. This is the personal allowance. Most people are employed, thereby paying their tax weekly or monthly under PAYE.

Index Fund

A portfolio of investments that are weighted the same as a stock-exchange index in order to mirror its performance. This process is also referred to as indexing. Investing in an index fund is known as passive investing. The primary advantage to such a strategy is the lower management expense ratios on index funds. Also, the majority of collective investments fail to beat broad indexes such as the FTSE All Share.

Individual Savings Account (ISA)

In the UK, an Individual Savings Account (ISA) is a scheme allowing individuals to hold shares, unit trusts, and cash, free of tax on dividends, interest, and capital gains; in 1999 it replaced both Personal Equity Plans (PEPs) and Tax-Exempt Special Savings Accounts (TESSAs).

Inheritance Tax (IHT)

In the event of your death, this tax may be payable by your heirs, but bear in mind: transfers between a husband and wife are exempt, provided they are both domiciled within the UK. There is no tax to pay on the first portion of your estate (the nil-rate band). In practice, if you're a homeowner, even with only modest other assets, thanks to rampant house-price inflation there's still a good chance you'll fall into the tax net. But careful tax planning and a properly drawn up Will can play a key role in avoiding or minimising the tax that will eventually be due. The easiest way to mitigate your IHT liability is to give away some of your assets. IHT has been called a *voluntary tax* because there are so many ways you can give money away exempt from tax, or potentially exempt — but make sure you keep within the rules.

Insurance Bonds

Sometimes referred to as *investment bonds*, these are single-premium savings contracts issued by life insurance companies. The investor hands over his money to a fund manager, who uses his expertise to make the investment grow as quickly as possible. Bonds can offer useful income flexibility and can be particularly useful in planning Inheritance Tax because they can be written under trust. Insurance bonds can typically be broken down into four categories: Managed Bonds, With-Profits Bonds, Equity Bonds and Distribution Bonds.

Interest-only Mortgages

An interest-only mortgage is a loan on which you pay no more than the interest charged. In effect, you are merely servicing the debt, not reducing it. The amount you owe remains constant. If you have an interest-only mortgage, the onus is on you to arrange how to repay the capital at the end of the mortgage term. Most borrowers with these types of loan take out some kind of long-term savings plan such as an endowment policy or Individual Savings Account (ISA).

Intestacy

If you die without making a Will (dying *intestate*), the law dictates how your estate will be passed on. The law aims, in the first instance, to protect your immediate family — husband or wife, and children. This might be exactly what you had wished, but even if it was, dying without a Will might not result in your possessions (your estate) being used as you had expected or would have wished.

Investment Trusts

Investment trusts are companies which invest in the shares of other companies. They are collective investments which pool together the money of many investors. This money is then invested in a portfolio (or wide range) of companies which will be more varied than the small investor could achieve on his own. There are a number of key differences between unit trusts and investment trusts.

Kabbalah

The ancient Jewish tradition of mystical interpretation of the Bible, first transmitted orally and using esoteric methods (including ciphers). It reached the height of its influence in the later Middle Ages.

Letter of Wishes

Where a trust document gives the trustees very wide powers and discretions a Settlor may provide the trustees with a letter, commonly known as a Letter of Wishes. This letter principally sets out the manner in which the Settlor wishes the trustees to exercise their powers and discretions, but is not binding on the trustees. All binding requirements must be contained in the trust document.

Long-Term Care (LTC)

Insurance to cover long-term care has long been a feature of financial services in the United States, but it was not until 1992 that the cover was launched in the UK. Long-term care benefit may be used to provide care, either at home, or on a part-time or full-time basis in a residential or nursing home. Average annual nursing home costs are now estimated at around £ 24,000 a year for full-time care. The alternative to having your assets eaten up by care costs is long-term care insurance. Such policies pay out when the insured party can no longer perform a number of daily living functions without assistance.

Mutual Funds

These are often described as the American equivalent of unit trusts.

National Insurance Contributions

National insurance is a form of tax which everyone in work must pay in order to qualify for benefits, including the State pension. Most employed people pay Class 1 contributions, which entitle you to incapacity benefit, jobseeker's allowance, maternity allowance, retirement pension and widow's pension (if you meet the right qualifying conditions). If you are self-employed you have to pay two sets of NI. They are known as Class 2 (which give you rights to the State pension, maternity benefit, incapacity benefit and widow's benefit) and Class 4 contributions (for which you receive no benefits).

National Savings

The Department of National Savings is a Government department which has the role of bringing in extra cash to help the Government pay its bills. Put another way, the department is another way for the Treasury to raise money to help meet the shortfall in the Government's income. It's been described as the Government's little piggy bank, but the serious role of National Savings is to borrow money from you and me by selling us competitive investment products.

Nil Rate Band

The law allows you to leave an estate worth up to £ 263,000 (tax year 2004/5, previously £ 255,000 for 2003/4) without having to pay any Inheritance Tax upon it. This £ 263,000 is called the nil-rate-band. After the first £ 263,000, or the nil-rate-band, the remainder of your estate will be charged 40% Inheritance Tax. Each person has a nil-rate-band, which creates planning opportunities for couples.

Occupational Pension Schemes

You are not legally obliged to join an employer's occupational pension scheme. However, most of the time, if such a scheme is offered it makes sense to do so. Your employer's plan may also provide other benefits, such as: life insurance cover while you are in employment; a pension if you are forced to retire early due to ill health; a pension for your dependants when you die; an increase to your pension every year once you start receiving your pension; and also, your employer is likely to pay the administration costs of the plan.

Offshore Funds

These are collective investments which are based in overseas places, typically Dublin, Jersey, Guernsey, Isle of Man, Luxembourg and Bermuda.

Open Ended Investment Company (OEIC)

OEICs are pooled investment vehicles, in company form. They are like unit trusts which they are designed to replace. They are the norm internationally and the UK is now coming into line in an effort to open these foreign markets to UK companies.

Par Value

Government gilts are issued with a par value of £ 100 and, as they are traded on the market throughout their lives, their value can vary above or below £ 100 depending on their popularity at the time. When they reach their redemption date they will be redeemed at their par value of £ 100.

Passive Management

An investing strategy that mirrors a market index and does not attempt to beat the market. Also known as passive strategy or passive investing.

Pay As You Earn (PAYE)

PAYE is the system by which the tax man collects revenue from people who are employed — in other words, working for an organisation which pays them a salary. The income tax due is deducted at source and then passed on to the Inland Revenue. This mechanism for bringing in tax is liked by the Inland Revenue because it effectively means employers act as unpaid tax collectors. The onus on seeing that the correct amount of tax is paid is on the employer.

Penny Shares

The Financial Services Authority (FSA) designate penny shares as shares which have limited liquidity - in other words, that are hard to buy and sell in quantity without moving the price. Specifically, the FSA singled out those with a spread of 10% or more between buying and selling prices. The FSA definition highlights one of the dangers of penny shares: in order to make a profit on them, you need a significant rise in share price just to cover the wide spread. Novice investors often make the mistake of equating low share price with value. That's a fundamental error.

Pensionable Salary

The earnings on which benefits and/or contributions are calculated. One or more elements of earnings (for example, overtime) may be excluded.

Permanent Health Insurance (PHI)

Many people believe that should they fall ill and be unable to work, the State will look after them. However, in recent times the Government has shifted the onus of providing an income during illness increasingly onto the shoulders of the individual. Permanent health insurance (PHI) typically provides a monthly income during periods of long-term illness or disability. It is also commonly referred to as *income protection cover, disability insurance and income replacement cover.*

Permanent Interest Bearing Shares (PIBs)

Issued by major building societies, these offer investors a set income paid twice yearly, net of basic rate tax. Traded on the London Stock Exchange, their capital value moves in response to interest rates. If rates rise, the capital value reflected in the buying price falls and vice versa.

Personal Equity Plans (PEPs)

As of 6 April 1999, PEPs were closed for new business. You cannot now put any more money into a PEP. However, investments made within PEPs prior to that date continue to benefit from the tax shelter. You may also, of course, invest further funds in an Individual Savings Account (ISA) which replaced PEPs.

Potentially Exempt Transfer (PET)

A potentially exempt transfer is one which will become exempt once the donor has lived for seven years from the date of the gift. If he or she does not survive seven years then the gift is subject to inheritance tax, but 'taper relief' may reduce the impact.

Power of Attorney

A document which gives a person the right to make binding decisions for another, as an agent. A Power of Attorney may be specific to a certain kind of decision or general, in which the agent makes all major decisions for the person who is the subject of the Power of Attorney. The person signing the Power of Attorney is usually referred to, in law, as the Donor and the person that would exercise the Power of Attorney, the Donee.

Private Medical Insurance (PMI)

This insurance is designed to pay the cost of treatment for any medical condition which falls within the cover taken out. This can include surgery such as coronary by-passes, hernia repairs and hip replacements. Private medical insurance is unlikely to cover long-term illnesses or degenerative diseases brought on by old age.

Progressive Life Planning

An interactive process that engages the client by asking questions that address what they want their money to do, such as 'what makes you really happy?' and 'what is important about money to you?' Through this level of engagement, clients gain a personal framework for decision-making that enables them to make better financial choices, and so they have a sense of control over their financial affairs.

Qualifying Insurance Policy

The benefit of a qualifying policy is that there will be no further tax to pay on the 'pay out', provided it is kept going for at least 10 years. This is especially good news for a higher-rate taxpayer who would face an extra tax charge on gains from the policy if it were *non-qualifying*. There is a set of rules which determine whether a policy is *qualifying*. For instance, for an endowment policy to be qualifying, it needs to be kept in place for three-quarters of the term, if this is less than 10 years. It is best to ask the insurer or your professional adviser whether a policy is qualifying.

Rebalancing

The process of realigning the weightings of one's portfolio of assets. For example, if your portfolio's proportion of equities has grown too large for your intended assets weightings, you might rebalance by selling some stock and putting it into cash or fixed-interest securities (Government gilts or corporate bonds).

Regular Savings Scheme

While investing in the stock market was once only the province of the wealthy with considerable lump sums to invest, the advent of the regular savings scheme has meant that this is no longer the case. Besides making equity investment accessible to those of slender means, regular savings schemes have a number of other advantages. The fact that you are dripping your money gradually into the investment, rather than all in one go, means that you don't need to worry about market timing and the risk of buying shares just at the moment when they are wildly overpriced and are about to plummet in value. Also, regular savers benefit from an effect called *pound/cost averaging*, which means that, over time, the average amount paid for the shares works out to be less than the share's average price.

Remortgage

This is simply the replacement of an existing mortgage with a new one. You may do this to save money. This might be possible by switching to another mortgage product with the same lender or by switching your business to a competitor. Remember, if you switch lenders, the saving you make on the interest rate you pay may be partially or wholly eaten up by the transaction charges associated with moving your loan.

Self Invested Personal Pensions (SIPPs)

These are personal pensions plans in which the person saving for retirement has the flexibility to make their own investment decisions. If you choose this route, you'll be confronted with a range of options about what to invest in. However, this approach will only make sense for people investing several thousand pounds a year, otherwise the charges are likely to outweigh the benefits.

Settlor

The Settlor of a trust is the person who establishes that trust i.e. the person who gives the money or policy in the first place.

Sufism

Sufism is the esoteric dimension of the Islamic faith, the spiritual path to mystical union with God. It is influenced by other faiths, such as Buddhism, and reached its peak in the 13th century. There are many Sufi orders, the best-known being the dervishes.

Taper Relief (Capital Gains Tax)

Its purpose is to reduce the amount of capital gains tax you have to pay when you sell shares, to account for the effect of inflation.

Taper Relief (Inheritance Tax)

A sliding scale which can reduce the tax payable where a person dies within seven years of having made a potentially exempt transfer (PET).

Tax Exempt Special Savings Account (TESSA)

In the UK, a Tax-Exempt Special Savings Account allowing savers to invest a certain amount in a bank or building society with no tax to pay on the interest, provided that the capital remains in the account for five years (replaced in 1999 by the ISA).

Term Assurance

Term assurance is the most straightforward and the cheapest form of life insurance. It offers cover for a specified number of years. It is most often used to cover a long-term loan such as a mortgage. This form of cover tends to be much cheaper than whole life policies because you are only being given cover for a number of years. If you live to the end of the term, you will receive nothing.

The Institute of Financial Planning (IFP)

The Institute exists 'to set the standards in ethics and education for financial planners of all disciplines'. It argues that financial planning is a scientific process, aimed at first identifying your goals in life before trying to satisfy your needs with financial products.

Tracker Fund

A type of collective investment (unit trust, investment trust, OEIC) that provides the same returns as an index. The fund invests in all the companies within the index according to a market value weighting. A tracker fund is virtually the same as an index fund.

Traded Endowment Policy (TEP)

With TEPs you choose the tax treatment best suited to your circumstances. This can be achieved by selecting a qualifying policy that is subject to capital gains tax, allowing you to use your annual tax allowance to soak up any gain. However, you could select a non-qualifying policy. The proceeds will be tax free to basic-rate taxpayers. Higher-rate taxpayers will probably have to pay some tax, but will benefit from a complex mitigation opportunity known as top slicing. The subject requires professional help.

Trust

A fiduciary relationship in which one person, a trustee, holds title to property or assets for the benefit of another person, the beneficiary.

Unit Trusts

Unit trusts are collective investments which give modest and not-so-modest private investors a chance to make capital gains, usually by investing in the stockmarket. Unit trusts offer investors the potential to achieve capital gains, but this option entails taking a degree of added risk. However, some of the risk may have been minimised, because when you put your money into a unit trust, you are effectively buying a small quantity of shares in several companies. Precisely which companies are chosen will be decided by the fund manager.

Venture Capital Trust (VCT)

The Venture Capital Trust scheme started on 6 April 1995. It is designed to encourage individuals to invest indirectly in a range of small higher-risk trading companies whose shares and securities are not listed on a recognised stock exchange, by investing through Venture Capital Trusts (VCTs). So, if you invest in a VCT, you spread the investment risk over a number of companies. If you invest in them you may be entitled to various income tax and capital gains tax reliefs.

Weighted Index

A stockmarket index, in which each stock affects the index in proportion to its market value. Also called capitalisation weighted index, examples include the FTSE 100, the S&P 500, and the Hang Seng Index.

Whole of life Policy

This is an insurance policy that covers you for the entirety of your life. People often take out whole of life policies so that, after their death, their beneficiaries will receive a lump sum. This might be used to pay off debts or even an inheritance tax bill. When you buy a whole of life policy, bear in mind that the regular premiums you're paying are not fixed for the lifetime of the policy. From time to time (every 10 years or more), the life insurer reserves the right to increase the premium you pay.

Resources

I have put together a list of further reading and information sources, which I think you may find interesting to explore.

BOOKS

Goals!
Brian Tracy
Berrett-Koehler Publishers, Inc

Life is a Four Letter Word
Roger Holmes Wood CFP
1st Books

Motivation and Goal-Setting (second edition)

National Press Publications

Career Press

Now, Discover Your Strengths

Marcus Buckingham and Donald Clifton

Simon & Schuster

Seven Stages of Money Maturity

George Kinder

Random House, Inc

So You Want to Be a Financial Planner

Nancy Langdon Jones

AdvisorPress

Soar with Your Strengths

Donald O Clifton and Paula Nelson

Delacorte Press

Sudden Money: Managing a Financial Windfall

Susan Bradley and Mary Martin

John Wiley & Sons

The Money Tracker

Judy Lawrence

AdvisorPress

The New Retirementality

Mitch Anthony

Dearborn Trade

Your Clients for Life –
The Definitive Guide to Becoming a Successful Financial Life Planner
Mitch Anthony
Dearborn Trade Publishing

MAGAZINES

The Economist (weekly)
www.economist.com

WEBSITES

Financial Services Authority (FSA) — consumer information
www.fsa.gov.uk/consumer/index.html

The Institute of Financial Planning
www.financialplanning.org.uk

TrustNet — investment funds information service
www.trustnet.co.uk

Financial Times — Your Money
www.ftyourmoney.co.uk

The Pension Service
Part of the Department for Work and Pensions
www.thepensionservice.gov.uk

Guardian Unlimited
http://money.guardian.co.uk

Bob Veres (US subscription service for financial professionals only)

www.bobveres.com

Kinder Institute of Life Planning

www.kinderinstitute.com

Mitch Anthony's Institute of Financial Life Planning

www.flpinc.com

TRADEMARKED TERMS

The following terms in this book are trademarked by The WealthFlow Partnership:

WealthFlow™; The WealthFlow System™; Progressive Life Planning & Management™; Breakthrough Cash & Credit Management™; Personal Risk Management Programme™; Savings, Investment & Risk Integration™; Retirement & Life Transition Management™; Tax Planning & Mitigation Programme™; and Estate Planning & Management Programme™.

What Did You Think?

It's been a huge adventure getting this book together and I would love to know what you think of it, and whether you're considering taking the financial life planning journey yourself as a result.

Please send your feedback to me, Duncan R Glassey, at The WealthFlow Partnership,

83 Princes Street
Edinburgh
EH2 2ER
Scotland
United Kingdom

Telephone 0131 247 6745

feedback@wealthflow.org
www.wealthflow.org

Please email me at newsletter@wealthflow.org to sign up for my free monthly e-zine. It's full of tips on financial life planning – and special offers on books. There's also news about courses and e-books, some of them free.

Special Acknowledgement - Mitch Anthony

I am very grateful for the opportunity to benefit from the ground-breaking work of Mitch Anthony in the US. An example of this being the 'Life Transitions Profile' recorded in the appendix (copyright 2004, Financial Life Planning Institute). Mitch has also served to provide inspiration to develop a range of client centred questions, including: Are you satisfied with your current job/career? Are you satisfied with the income/benefits you receive from your current job/career? Are you satisfied with your spending habits? Are you satisfied with your ability to meet your financial obligations?

Mitch Anthony is the founder of the Financial Life Planning Institute and is the founder and President of Advisor Insights, Inc., a firm specializing in training financial service professionals in relationship building skills. Mitch is the author of several books for financial advisers, including *StorySelling for Financial Advisors, The New Retirementality, Your Clients for Life, Selling With Emotional Intelligence* and most recently, *Your Clients Story* (available Spring, 2005). Mitch's work has been featured on *ABC Evening News with Peter Jennings, CNN, Bloomberg, CBS Marketwatch, Kiplingers Magazine,* and many other media outlets. His radio program, The Daily Dose, is heard daily on 170 radio stations nationwide.

"Financial Life Planning places the life of the client at the heart of the financial planning process.

Financial Life Planning is about coming to the right answers by asking the right questions. This involves broadening the conversation beyond investment selection and asset management to exploring life issues as they relate to money. Financial Life Planning is an approach that integrates qualitative aspects of a client's life with quantitative aspects of their financial situation.

Financial Life Planning is an organized process that helps the adviser move his or her practice from financial transaction thinking to life transition thinking. The first step is to help clients *see* the connection between their financial lives and the challenges and opportunities inherent in each life transition.

The Financial Life Planning process provides discovery dialogues on History, Principles, Transitions and Goals. These are the four cornerstones of the client's life. With the Financial Life Planning process advisers can not only gather and store qualitative client information to integrate into the financial plan but can produce personalized financial life reports for clients as well. The Financial Life Planning model positions the adviser as a Partner, Guide and Educator in the lives of the clients they serve."

Mitch Anthony, November 2004
www.flpinc.com

Printed in the United Kingdom
by Lightning Source UK Ltd.
125620UK00001B/3-50/A